DARRIN BREGE   KAREN BELL-BREGE
SKETCH THE MYTHS

ISBN 978-0-9774119-7-9

The trademark Five Ways to Finish® is registered in the U.S. Patent and Trademark Office.
The trademark Ghost Board Posse® is registered in the U.S. Patent and Trademark Office.

Printed in the United States of America
First Printing Paperback Edition – November 2010

Published by: Team B Creative
9864 E. Grand River Ave,
Suite 110, No, 244, Brighton, MI 48116

Graphics, Layout/Design Darrin Brege
Written by Karen Bell-Brege & Darrin Brege
Copyediting by Teresa McGee, 22 House Writing Works, NY, NY.

Foreword by Josh Linkner, Founder & Chairman, ePrize
Author of Disciplined Dreaming: A Proven System to Drive Breakthrough Creativity

Special thanks to Matt Busch, Star Wars Illustrator and Professor, Macomb College

Printed by McNaughton & Gunn, Inc.
Saline, MI USA
December 2010

www.mickmorris.com
www.ghostboardposse.com

To those of you who love art (in any format) and know its value and importance in our world – this book is for you! Although, some people no longer realize the importance of art and creating – if you look back through the ages you will see how truly important art is. So, if it's your desire to create, and that is what is in your heart...then you must go for it, because remember...It starts with art!

-The Breges

Gremlin - by Mick, age 14

SKETCH THE MYTHS

TABLE OF CONTENTS:

FOREWORD

Darrin and Karen Brege have done it again! In Sketch the Myths, the Breges creativity shines and yours will too. This easy-to-follow guide offers a roadmap of creative inspiration and allows you to blossom as an artist. It provides a wonderful family activity for "kids" of all ages (including 40+ year olds like me!). I have been inspired by Darrin and Karen for years, and their drive to help make the world a more creative planet. This fun, engaging work is one of their best and I highly encourage you to buy and enjoy it.

As the complexity of the world increases, so does the need for creativity. Unfortunately, schools tend to beat that creativity out of kids instead of nurturing it. This book is an important step in unleashing your creativity and helping to build your imagination.   I'm excited to enjoy the book with my own kids, and highly encourage you to do the same. The future of business (and life) will be about creative expression and original thought. We need more books like this to enable our kids to succeed in the future. A future with increasing speed, complexity, and competition.

Enjoy this amazing book, and you will benefit for years to come. Thanks to Darrin and Karen for bringing Sketch the Myths to life. It is a great contribution to the world.

Josh Linkner
Founder & Chairman, ePrize
Author, *Disciplined Dreaming:*
A Proven System to Drive Breakthrough Creativity

ABOUT DARRIN

I was born in Michigan and lived there most of my life. I started drawing when I was just three years old. I continued to draw through all of my years in school. After graduating from High School, I went to Albion College. I graduated from Albion and then I moved to Los Angeles and studied at the Motion Picture Screen Cartoonists in North Hollywood. When the 1994 earthquake hit in Southern California, it was an easy decision to move back to Michigan where I worked for a company creating animated storybook CD-ROMs for companies like Disney and Hasbro Interactive. Best of all, I auditioned for Karen's improv troupe and joined – performing weekly for over a decade. Karen and I fell in love, got married and had a son (Mick), who is the namesake for our *Mick Morris Myth Solver* books. Besides our books, I work as a Creative Director; where I am fortunate to work on promotions for over 75 of the top 100 brands in the world. I have also been a comedic impressionist on the radio for many years. Karen and I (and sometimes Mick) love to visit schools and libraries every year inspiring, teaching and making children laugh - and I can't imagine a better career.

ABOUT KAREN

I was born in Michigan, but spent much of my life living in foreign countries when I was young, and then moved to different states when I finished college. My degree was in broadcasting and communications and I started out as a Radio Announcer in Ocean City, Maryland. There, I was asked to write some advertising copy, and before I knew it I was offered a job as a copywriter for a television station. I ended up moving back to Michigan and worked as a Fashion Commentator, a Copywriter and a Communications Specialist, and also started a comedy troupe at Mark Ridley's Comedy Castle...as you know that's how I met Darrin. We got married and had our son, Mick. Darrin began illustrating the covers of the Chillers books (original covers) and then we were asked to write and illustrate the The Chill Art Sketchbook. Our son Mick was 8 years old, so we decided that we should do our own book series, making Mick the namesake. Thus, the *Mick Morris Myth Solver* books were started. I love writing books, copy - everything, and getting to work with such a fantastic artist as Darrin, I consider myself very, very lucky!

The Canton Observer interviewed Darrin for this article in 1981.

GARY CASKEY/staff photographer
Darren Brege, 13, uses his vivid imagination to create comic-book characters which he calls "freakies."

8

INTRODUCTION

Hello fellow artists! That's right, you are an artist. Anyone who likes to create in any way – whether it be drawing, painting, sculpting, designing, (including other artistic endeavors such as: writing, singing, acting, playing a musical instrument) has the right to call themselves an artist. Karen and I feel that art is such an important part of life, because imagine if there wasn't any! How totally boring would everything be?

Now, some of you know me as the artist for the *Mick Morris Myth Solver* and *Ghost Board Posse* book series (and I also did all of the original art for the Michigan and American Chillers). I've done some other books along the way, too. But, this book is one of my favorites, and I know that you're gonna love it – because this is where I show you how to draw some scary, fun creatures!

You know, that the *Mick Morris Myth Solver* and *Ghost Board Posse* book series are filled with some frightening myth monsters, ghosts and zombies. For every one of those books, I get to work with the author, Karen Bell-Brege (who is also my wife – and we feel pretty lucky to get to work together). Before I even begin the art for the book, we research, and then decide what the creature should look like, how scary it should be, what should go in the background, the colors of the cover, and more. There is a lot of thought that goes into artwork…and this is exactly what I am going to teach you in this exciting book.

I'll show you how to design and sketch these images, plus how to come up with your very own style. I'll explain that no matter what it is you want to draw – every sketch starts with a simple stick figure. You'll learn about adding shapes, perspective, outlining, and detailing. Also, I will share with you some of the many tips and secrets that I've learned throughout my career as an artist. In fact, pssst…here's a secret for you right now…if you want to be a great artist, you have to practice, practice, practice…so what are we waiting for? Let's get going and Sketch the Myths!

Thank goodness my mom saved a bunch of my drawings when I was a kid. See the spider drawing below? That is my first recognizable drawing when I was 3 years old. The one on the left is something I called "Stone Age vs Space Age" featuring Fred and Dino from the Flintstones against Darth Vader and a Stormtrooper. It's from 1977, when I was nine. We featured it in our first book, and I've been asked how I would draw the same characters today. Well, here is my new sketch!

9

BUILDING A SKETCH

Okay, before we really get into the drawing techniques I use, it might help to show how the process gets broken down. When we do school visits, the first question I ask the audience is, "Who likes to draw?" The second is, "How many of you have built a house or castle out of blocks?" Naturally, almost every hand goes up. Just about every one of us has played with blocks at some point in our lives. And, we've probably stacked them up, which is a lot like building a house, because when you build a house, where do you start? At the bottom, right? You can't float a roof in mid-air and build down - unless you have magical powers. You start by building your base first, and continue upwards from there, putting your roof on last. To me, it's very similar to the drawing process. When you draw you're going to be starting at the bottom, and adding layer after layer. You'll keep the lines you want, and erase the ones you don't. So, instead of blocks, you're going to be starting with drawing basics - which you'll learn in the next few chapters. Specifically, begin with easy things like stick figures, shapes, and simple lines. These are all things we've been able to draw since we were very little... just about the same time that we were learning how to build things with blocks.

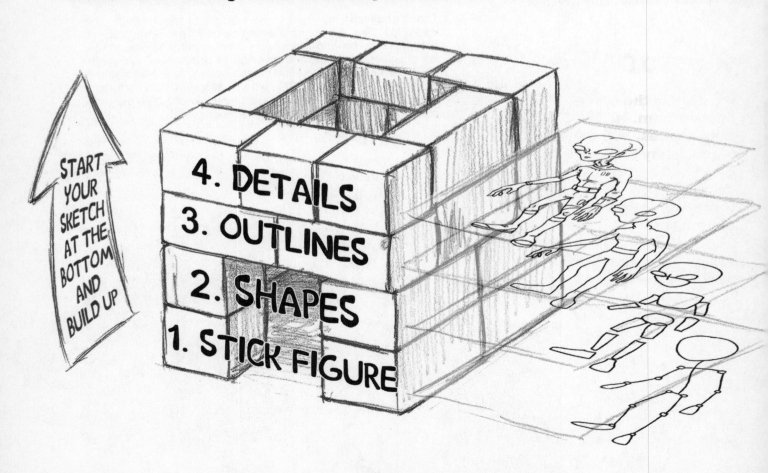

START YOUR SKETCH AT THE BOTTOM AND BUILD UP

4. DETAILS
3. OUTLINES
2. SHAPES
1. STICK FIGURE

GETTING STARTED - AN ARTIST'S TOOLS

Before you even begin to put pencil to paper, one of the most important elements of being an artist is using the proper tools and supplies...meaning paper, pencils, erasers, or a computer and the proper programs. I will give you suggestions and my tell you what my favorites are to use, but as you become more skilled you can decide what works best for you.

THE PERFECT PENCIL IS WHAT YOU'LL NEED!

To start sketching, the first thing you will need is a pencil. When you head to an art store you'll find that there is a huge selection to choose from, but don't worry about this when you first start out. Once you've mastered sketching, that's when you can look into the variety of pencils. Right now I suggest that you start with a basic pencil, one with a No. 2 lead, or you can use a disposable pencil – the kind that you find in packages at any office supply store. The disposable pencil is what I work with; I find it very easy to use, especially when I'm in the middle of a drawing. I don't have to stop to sharpen my pencil. Give it a try you might like it, or you may prefer a different pencil. Just remember, the right pencil for you is the one that you are most comfortable drawing with.

WHAT TO DRAW ON - PASS THE PAPER PLEASE

It's kind of the same thing as choosing a pencil, there is a huge variety of paper to choose from. You will be amazed by the shapes, sizes, colors, weights, textures and thicknesses. You can draw in a notebook, sketchbook or on single sheets of paper – which is my choice. I like the simplicity of using regular white copy paper in the 8 1/2 by 11 size. I find that if I don't like what I've drawn or want to start over, it's easy just to crumple it up, and toss it in the recycle bin (think green and recycle, please). Oh yeah, there are days when I crumple it up and throw it away...and that's okay. Except when I am really far into the drawing, then the most important thing to me is my eraser – but we'll get to that in a minute. If you do prefer a notebook or sketchbook, so that you can save your drawings neatly, just remember to make sure that the one you select has paper that erases easily. You don't want paper that smudges, smears or tears.

THE ERASER IS YOUR BEST FRIEND

Seriously, I'm not kidding, when it comes to being an artist the most important tool that you will ever use is the eraser. You really shouldn't use just any old pencil top eraser. You will need a kneaded rubber eraser and here's why: you don't want to have any smudges, smears, lines or marks left on your paper when you erase. A kneaded eraser is available at most art and craft supply stores. It is gray and shaped like a rectangle. When you take off the cellophane wrapper it will feel like clay and that's the fun part about it. You can make it in to any shape that you like!

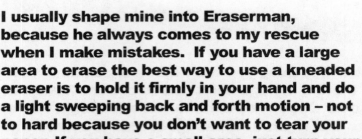

I AM ERASERMAN!
I CAN CLEAN UP
ANY JOB! SERIOUSLY....
ANYTHING YOU KNEAD.

I usually shape mine into Eraserman, because he always comes to my rescue when I make mistakes. If you have a large area to erase the best way to use a kneaded eraser is to hold it firmly in your hand and do a light sweeping back and forth motion – not to hard because you don't want to tear your paper. If you have a small area, just turn your kneaded eraser into a point and gently tap the area.

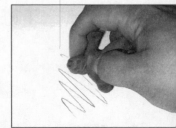

SWEEP

NOT JUST ANY OLD SURFACE FOR YOU

When drawing, especially if you are using single sheets of paper and not a sketchbook, remember that you really need to have a nice smooth surface. This may sound trivial, but if there are bumps and dents, or rims on the surface you are drawing on, it will really affect your art.

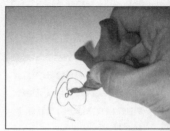

TAP

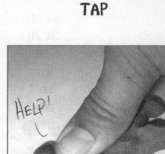

COMPUTERS AND PROGRAMS, THEY ARE OH, SO IMPORTANT IN ART THESE DAYS!

In the beginning, when you are just starting to draw, you really won't need a computer – but the more advanced you get you definitely will. I really, really, really (did I say really?) recommend that you learn how to use a computer, because if you do pursue a career as an artist you will have to use one.   For every drawing I do, when I am finished sketching I scan it in the computer. Once my drawing is onscreen I paint it in the computer. The program that I use is Photoshop. But there are countless other programs for artists, and I recommend you learn one. Of course, you don't have to do it my way, but if you are serious about being an artist – you will have to use a computer and know the various art programs.

THE STICK FIGURE – WHERE EVERY DRAWING BEGINS!

I know it sounds simple enough, drawing a stick figure. We all know it's so easy to do. Who would ever have thought that this is the foundation of drawing characters? A stick figure is made up of straight lines and circles – all of your myth creatures will come from these simple lines.

Let's give it a try. Try starting by drawing a human-shaped stick figure. Practice sketching them over and over in different sizes.

OKAY   GOOD   BEST

I'M A STICK! GO FIGURE.

You can see on my stick figures I have added little circles where the elbows, knees, hips and shoulders are. These circles indicate where the joints should be – just like on a human, allowing freedom of movement.

Terrific! Now that you are an expert at drawing stick figures, let's draw some and add the little round circles for joints...only this time try changing the position of the arms, legs, head and body. Try drawing them running, jumping, or sitting down.

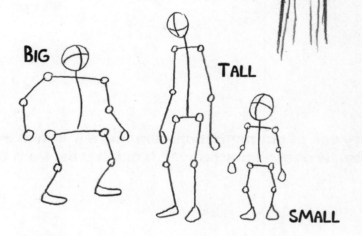

BIG   TALL   SMALL

Excellent! Now let's move on to drawing them in action poses!

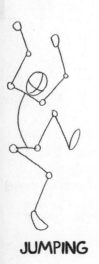

RUNNING

SITTING

JUMPING

STOP THAT YOU TWO!!

Practice makes perfect! Now that you are great at drawing simple stick figures, let's try changing your human drawing to a creature. To do this, start by changing the size of his shoulders by making them bigger, and try making the arms longer and the legs shorter.

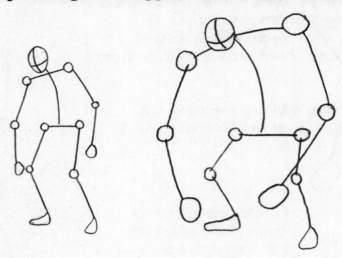

How's that for a change? Just by enlarging the basic shapes and adding different sizes we turned a stickman shape into something totally different. Now, it's big and starting to look scary!

Ready to try stick animals? Oh yeah, they start out as stick figures too.

Let's try a dog. Same thing, draw simple lines.

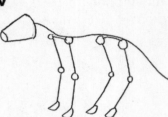

Now, let's try a bigger and more difficult animal, like an elephant.

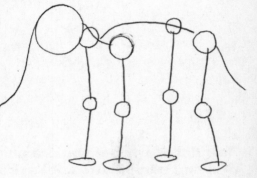

Every one of our myth monsters (even if drawn as a cartoon) started out as a simple stick figure. It doesn't matter which one it was, from Champ to Chupacabra...

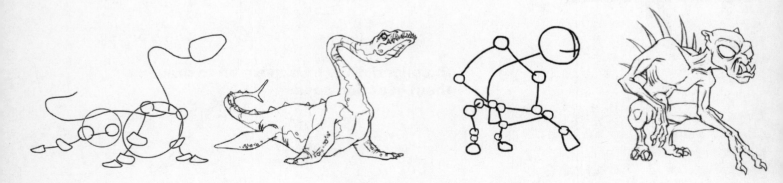

each and every one of the creepy beings started out as a simple line drawing.

Okay, shall we move on now that you have mastered drawing stick figures? Time for your drawing to get even better as we add shapes...this will change everything!

SHAPES - EVERYTHING IS TAKING SHAPE ALL AROUND US!

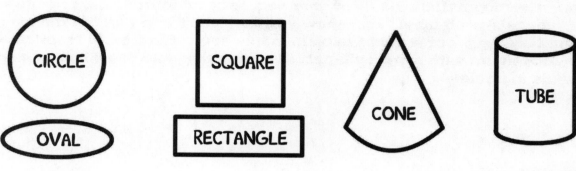

Above you can see six basic shapes.

Everywhere you look, no matter where you are everything is in a shape...even our planet! As you can see above, there are six basic shapes: a circle, an oval, a square, a rectangle, a cone and a tube. And when you look around, you can see that almost everything fits into one of these categories.

Let's have some fun! Right now, take a look around and see how many things you can find that fit these various shapes. How many did you find? Take for example your television – it's a rectangle, and your DVD player and remote control are too. The DVD is actually a circle, but it looks like an oval depending on the angle you look at it. Even an ice cream cone is a circle and a what? A cone – you got it!

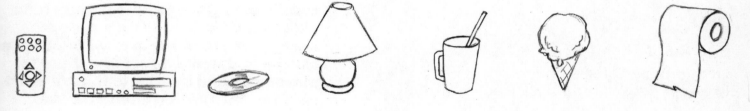

So, everything that we look at every day is one of these shapes or a combination of them. When you are drawing shapes, what is so important is that they are what give our myth creatures their thickness, bulk, size and dimension. Shapes give our monster mass!

Even the toilet paper tube is an important shape! And not just because it keeps our paper fresh, but because it is probably one of the most important shapes that we'll ever draw...no, I'm not kidding. Think about it, if you're drawing arms, legs, necks, tails and even hands...oh, and especially the fingers on the hands (because hands and fingers can be very hard to draw) knowing how to draw a toilet paper tube is of utmost importance. I know it sounds funny, but take a look at the next page...

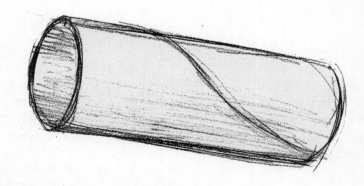

Okay, now I'll show you why being able to draw toilet paper tubes is so important. We'll start with the hand, because for me, hands were always a pain to draw. And hey, you can't go around putting mittens on all of your people or creatures...So, I had to figure out the best way to sketch them. As I show you how, you'll see that it's the same technique and building process that I explain in this book. First, we'll break down a hand in to a stick figure with simple shapes. Practice this, and you'll be drawing awesome hands in no time!

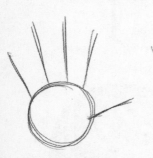

The stick figure hand. A circle and some sticks.

Now the shapes. Look at the palm of your hand. What do you see? Sort of a rectangle, and a couple of ovals.

Feel the bones in your thumb. There are two. So, two little toilet paper tubes. How about the fingers? Three. So, draw three little tubes.

Do you remember making a Thanksgiving Turkey by tracing your hand and adding details? Let's do the same. Now, trace around your shapes and tubes. Boom. You have a hand.

Certainly, if the fingers are holding something; or they are curled, pointing, or made to look like a claw, the tubes should be in perspective or facing you. (We'll show you that in the next couple of chapters.)

Now, let's imagine we have the same kind of hand we just drew with our stick figures and shapes...but it's a monstrous, giant hand coming over a cliff. It's time for a little lesson in energy. If you want to have fun with a sketch and make it feel like there is movement and energy to it, let's bend some lines. Curved lines give the appearance that things are in motion, even simple shapes. Think about your favorite sea sponge who's late for work and in a big hurry to get there. While he's running down the street, that rectangle (his body shape) is curved, showing movement. Straight lines in a sketch are pretty stiff, and typically boring. Here, we'll prove it to you...

Cliff Dweller A: Notice how stiff he's standing. He has no sense of urgency. No worry. Yawn.

Cliff Dweller B: Freaking out! Curved back. Frantic. Curved arms and legs. This person will make it back to the village to warn the others.
Cliff Dweller A: Not so much...it doesn't look good for him. You can see, even with simple stick figures, which one has the best chance of making it.

Now, fellow artists...get those hands moving. Bend some lines. Show some energy. Have some fun!

PERSPECTIVE – PICTURE IT FROM YOUR POINT OF VIEW...

Since we've just learned about shapes, now let's take them to a whole new level and look at them in 3 dimension, or as we know it 3D. This is being able to see things from another angle, when they are not flat. Take for example you are walking down a long empty hallway, maybe in your school or a building, it appears as if it goes on forever, but it doesn't. It's just your point of view.

See the drawing below, the doors at the far end are a good distance away. When we draw distance – like that, it's called perspective. As of now our myth creatures have gone from a stick figure to bulked up by adding shapes and objects. We also talked about the importance of having a dynamic pose to show movement and energy. To do this, some parts of your creature are going to look closer than others. Here are a couple quick lessons on perspective - don't skip this, it's important.

ONE POINT PERSPECTIVE

Let's go back to the hallway...remember it went on forever, from where you're standing it would look like the walls, floor and ceiling would all come to one point. That is called your vanishing point. This is the place where every line ends by coming together. Also, that point lands on what is called the horizon line; which is just a fancy way of saying the level that your eyes are at. Horizontal lines always go from left to right (not up and down-those are called vertical lines) A good example is when the sun sets on the horizon.

The drawing below shows you the hallways with the horizon line, vanishing point and vertical lines.

HORIZON LINE

VANISHING POINT

How do we do that for our drawing? First, draw your eye level or horizon line (remember, a line going left and right). Mark your vanishing point on that line.

HORIZON LINE

VANISHING POINT

Let's see how a box would look in our perspective practice. Draw a square keeping the vertical and horizontal lines either up and down, or left and right.

Now here's the fun part: for all of the other lines on our square that we can see, use a ruler to draw a line that hits your vanishing point.

Draw a vertical line to complete your box or rectangle in perspective. You can do it!

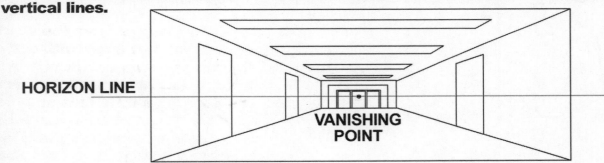

TWO POINT PERSPECTIVE:

This is the second part of our lesson on perspective – called Two Point Perspective. Again we will start by drawing a horizon line, but this time we will make two vanishing points. Don't forget that with one point perspective, our vertical and horizontal lines always stay the same. Now, the only lines that won't fade to the vanishing points are the vertical lines.

Try it yourself. Start by drawing your horizon line, and adding the two points.

Next, let's draw a vertical line.   Let's draw lines towards the vanishing points; both of them.

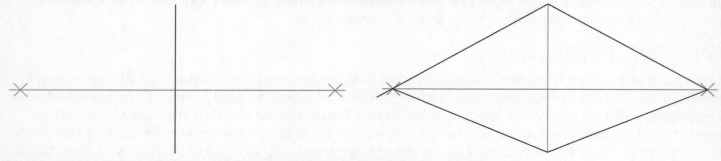

Add some more vertical lines to create the back edges to our box or building.

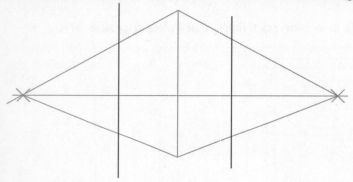

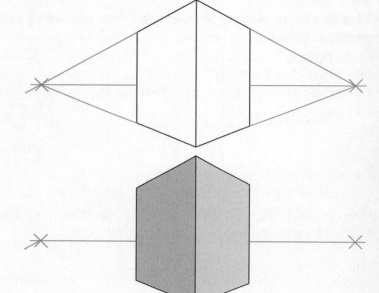

Draw a few more vertical lines, take them to the vanishing points, and we're close to making a city.

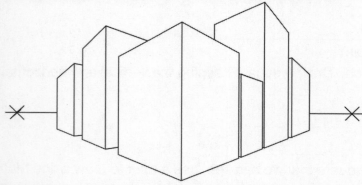

Perspective drawing takes lots of practice. So, to get good at it, you just need to keep practicing. One and two point perspective are the beginning steps in learning how to draw distance and depth – which is so important in making your drawing stand out.

Take for example, when a cover shows a myth from the story, we have to draw certain body parts, like arms and legs, to appear closer to you than others. Remember what we learned in our perspective work. Look at the Hodag from this book. Notice how its right front paw and tusk are slightly larger than the left front paw and tusk. We drew it bigger, to keep it in perspective. This way they're closer to our viewpoint. This is also called foreshortening; it makes a much more dynamic, realistic cover.

18

SHADING - WHAT LURKS IN THE SHADOWS?

Now that we've learned how shapes give our drawings dimension, it's time to add shading to really give our shapes form. But, before we start the shading process, we have to determine where our light source is coming from in our drawings. Is the light coming from above? Maybe, from the sun or moon, or is it underneath from a reflection off of water, or on the side from a window or lamp, or a flashlight? It's up to you to decide. But wherever you place your light source, it will affect your shading for everything in the drawing. Let's start out by simply shading our basic shapes.

HERE'S WHERE WE'LL PUT OUR LIGHT SOURCE!

The farther away an object is from light, the darker it's shading should be. On flat objects like our rectangle, the shading is a solid tone. It doesn't go from lighter to darker. That's not the case with smooth objects, on those we need to blend. Keep your hand loose and very lightly - scribble. To blend the shading and make it darker, scribble layers on top of what you've already scribbled. The more you scribble on layers, the darker it gets. Practice blending or gradient shading like this.

Okay, we've seen how the light can affect objects. Now it's time to see how the light affects where the objects are, or the surface that the objects rest upon. You'll need to keep this in mind when determining where your light source is - the higher the light is above your shapes or character, the shorter the length of the shadow will be on the ground. Think of how long your shadow looks at sunset, or from your porch light. But at noon, you'll cast much shorter shadows. When the light is directly above you, your shadow will be directly underneath you. Go ahead try this experiment by standing under a light source to see where your shadow is. Now try moving in different directions to see how your shadow is affected. This will give you a really good idea of shading with different light sources.

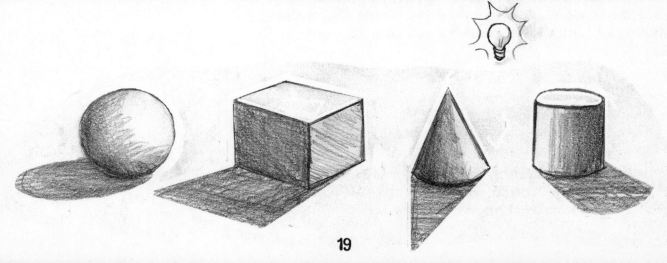

OUTLINING - THE CHAPTERS SO FAR...AND OUTLINES.

Whew...we've learned a lot of stuff. I know, I know, let's get to the monsters. We are almost there, I promise. Now would be a good time for a quick review of the last few chapters before we get drawing some myth monsters. Then, we'll move on to outlining. Just so you know, every cover, every creature, and even every little cartoon or sketch in this book was created using the following techniques.

So far, we've chosen our tools.

We posed out a stick figure.

We added simple shapes atop the stick figure.

Well, now what do we do? So far we've created the basic shapes and building blocks for our characters. The next step is outlining those shapes. This is where our eraser will come in handy. Once the outline is finished, we're going to erase the stick figure and the shapes. Erase what we've worked so hard to create?! Yes, we're pretty much through with them. Their purpose was to create the final outline. Then we'll be left with a shell of a character that needs to be detailed. Do we erase all of the guide lines? Well, some of the lines will be needed for details. Lines like the bottom of a jaw, face shapes, or the chest will remain.

Remember, the shapes helped show us the character's size. We don't want to directly draw our outline on top of them, but around them. The shapes simply guide our outline. Draw around them! When you finish erasing the various shapes and lines inside the outline, it will almost look like something out of a coloring book.

Note: Outlining is just like drawing a turkey by tracing around your hand, except you're tracing around the shapes you drew.

DETAILING - IT'S ALL IN THE DETAILS!

Here's where you really get to be creative and have fun, with this last step – detailing! Basically it's taking your outlined drawing, and adding the finishing touches. The things that will make it look real or scary. Detailing includes adding hats, clothes, props, fur, slime, scales, bumps, pimples, warts and even boogers. That's right - even boogers! You can detail your drawing with anything you want. It's up to you, but remember this...we artists are visual people. So, go online, hit the media center or library and look at images or videos of what you're trying to draw. If you're drawing a football player, it's probably a good idea to see what uniforms look like. The same goes for everything you're trying to visually represent, from guitars to background scenery. The details will make your sketch the best it can be – authentic and believable.

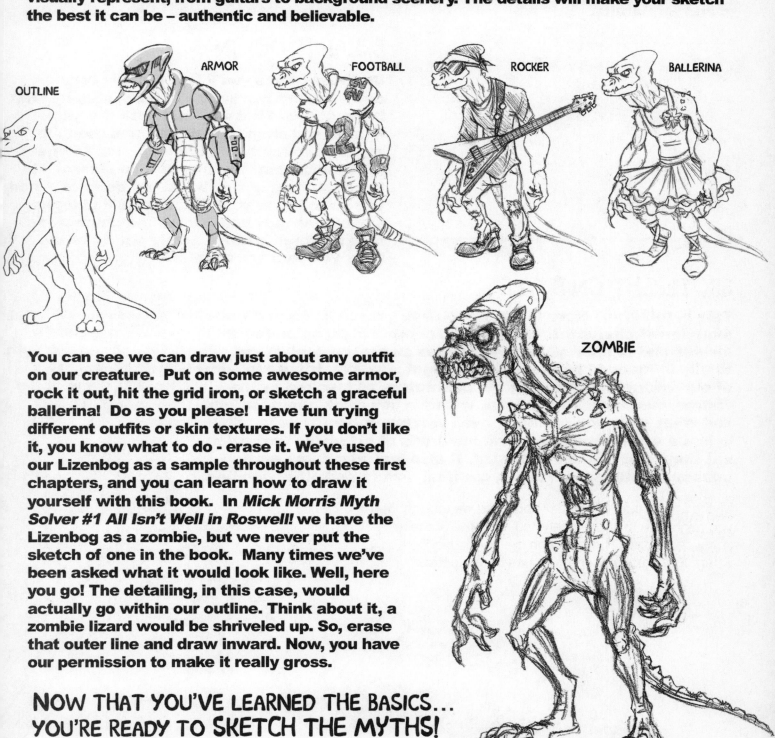

OUTLINE ARMOR FOOTBALL ROCKER BALLERINA

ZOMBIE

You can see we can draw just about any outfit on our creature. Put on some awesome armor, rock it out, hit the grid iron, or sketch a graceful ballerina! Do as you please! Have fun trying different outfits or skin textures. If you don't like it, you know what to do - erase it. We've used our Lizenbog as a sample throughout these first chapters, and you can learn how to draw it yourself with this book. In *Mick Morris Myth Solver #1 All Isn't Well in Roswell!* we have the Lizenbog as a zombie, but we never put the sketch of one in the book. Many times we've been asked what it would look like. Well, here you go! The detailing, in this case, would actually go within our outline. Think about it, a zombie lizard would be shriveled up. So, erase that outer line and draw inward. Now, you have our permission to make it really gross.

NOW THAT YOU'VE LEARNED THE BASICS... YOU'RE READY TO SKETCH THE MYTHS!

HOW TO FOLLOW THE NEXT 13 CHAPTERS:

ABOUT THE MYTHS

We've made this sketchbook pretty simple to follow. First, we give you some info on the myth itself; like where they originated, what the myth is supposed to look like and some info on human encounters. It's important to understand what you're drawing. And, the cool thing about these myth creatures – besides wondering if they really exist or not, is when you start to draw them you get to decide what you want to add for details.

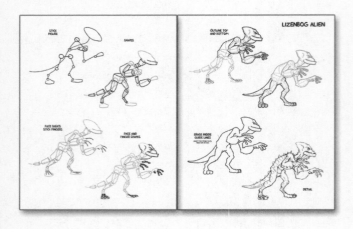

BREAK IT DOWN

On these pages you'll find that we break down the myth creature in easy, step-by-step instructions. First we start with the stick figures and shapes, outlines, and then we move on to the final detailing. Don't forget those important lessons that you learned in the beginning of this book. Remember, when you go to erase your initial building blocks, some lines may help define the character's face or other features. Only get rid of the lines you won't need later.

SPOTLIGHT ON STYLE

This is total fun! Here is where you will get to view a multitude of styles of characters from books, comic strips, animated movies and tv shows! We love movies and television! We're totally influenced by them, and thought we'd pay tribute to some of our favorites by drawing our characters as inspired by the various mediums. This is what will help you think about variety, and what style you prefer, or even what your own style is. This is just a small sampling of the hundreds of art styles that exist, but they're at the top of our list. It also features some early concept sketches, cartoons, our final covers and other doodles.

Myths are so cool to wonder about, so we thought that you might like to know where to find some of these scary creatures. The maps on the pages highlight where that particular creature has been spotted.

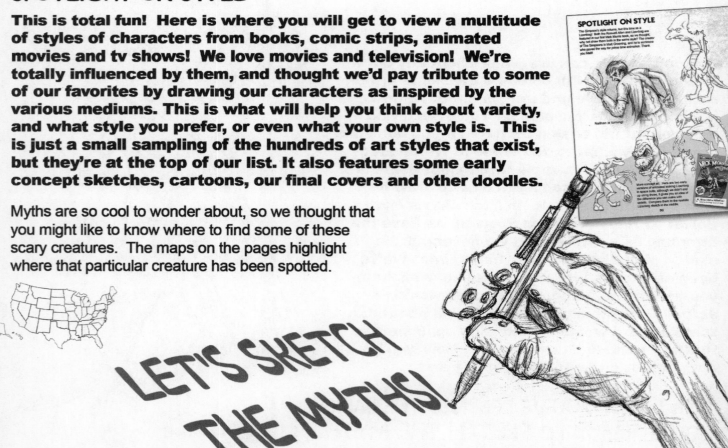

LET'S SKETCH THE MYTHS!

ROSWELL ALIEN

In the 1940's it was said that a mysterious spacecraft crashed to earth scattering little, grey alien bodies across the terrain. It happened on a ranch, and the owner immediately notified the nearest army base in Roswell, New Mexico – known as Area 51. The government was on the crash site instantly to investigate. Right away they declared the area as off limits; although they said that it was just a weather balloon and they were cleaning up the remnants. The military base and much of its surroundings also became a restricted area. And, the rancher and the local townspeople could no longer speak about what they saw – within hours they began to deny anything about it to the press. Before long, men in black suits were swarming the area. Since then, thousands and thousands of Unidentified Flying Objects (UFO's) have been reported across the globe. So, are there aliens? Some say absolutely, that these little grey-green men exist – others are non-believers. The strange thing about it is many ancient civilizations have similar carvings in their caves, their temples and pyramids of what present day aliens are described to look like: short with enormous heads, bulging, large black angular eyes, and about 3 feet tall. Many people even claim that they have been abducted by alien beings...Guess you'll have to decide for yourself...Do you believe?

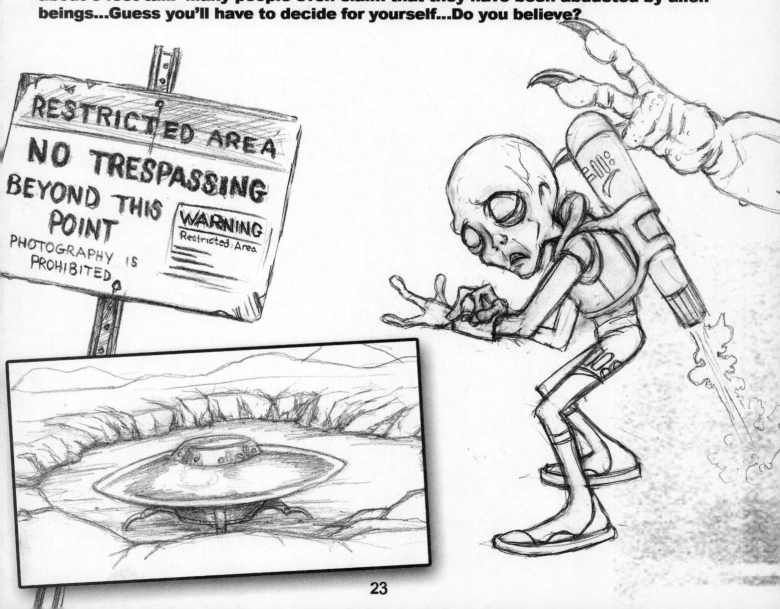

RESTRICTED AREA

NO TRESPASSING
BEYOND THIS POINT
PHOTOGRAPHY IS PROHIBITED

WARNING
Restricted Area

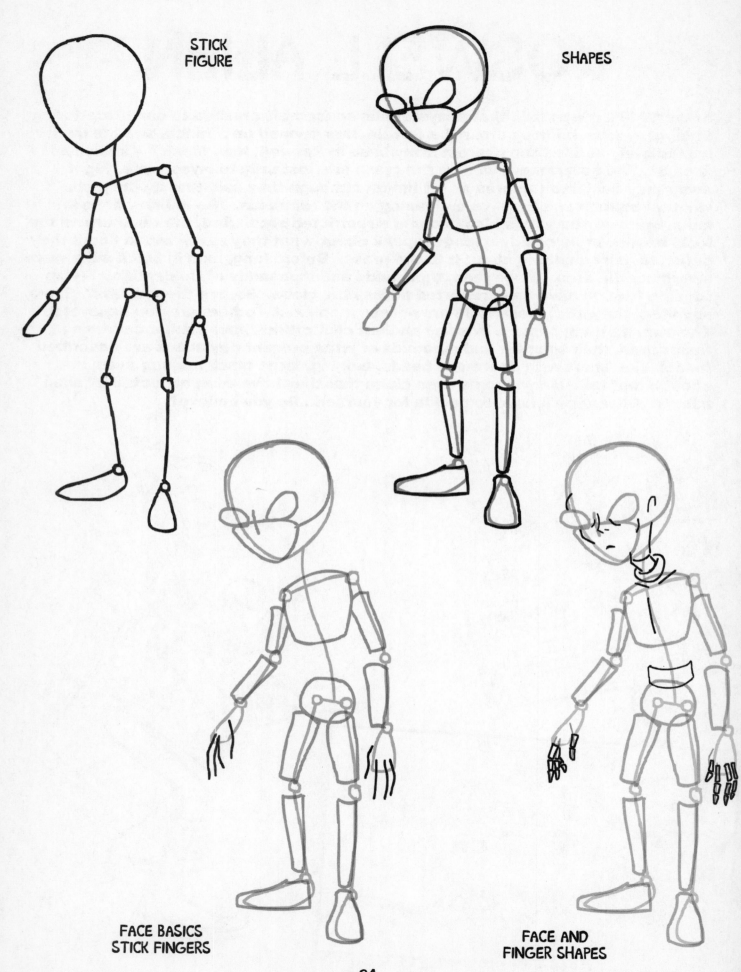

STICK
FIGURE

SHAPES

FACE BASICS
STICK FINGERS

FACE AND
FINGER SHAPES

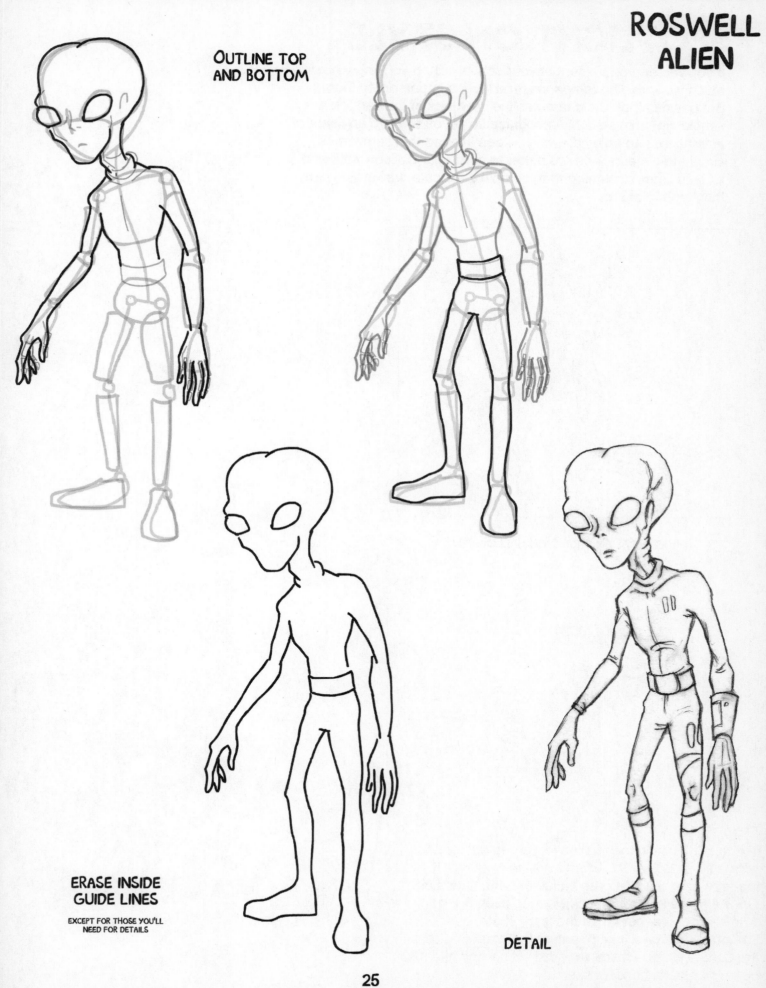

OUTLINE TOP
AND BOTTOM

ROSWELL
ALIEN

ERASE INSIDE
GUIDE LINES

EXCEPT FOR THOSE YOU'LL
NEED FOR DETAILS

DETAIL

SPOTLIGHT ON STYLE

If you've seen us present at your school – then you know how much we love *The Simpsons* (and love to impersonate them)! But besides that, the character line drawings of the cartoon are simple, yet unmistakably recognizable. If you are into any type of animation, and enjoy drawing – keep in mind that sometimes simple and clean lines are better to build your cartoon with, and a lot less time consuming than complex, intricate drawings – plus, they're funnier too!

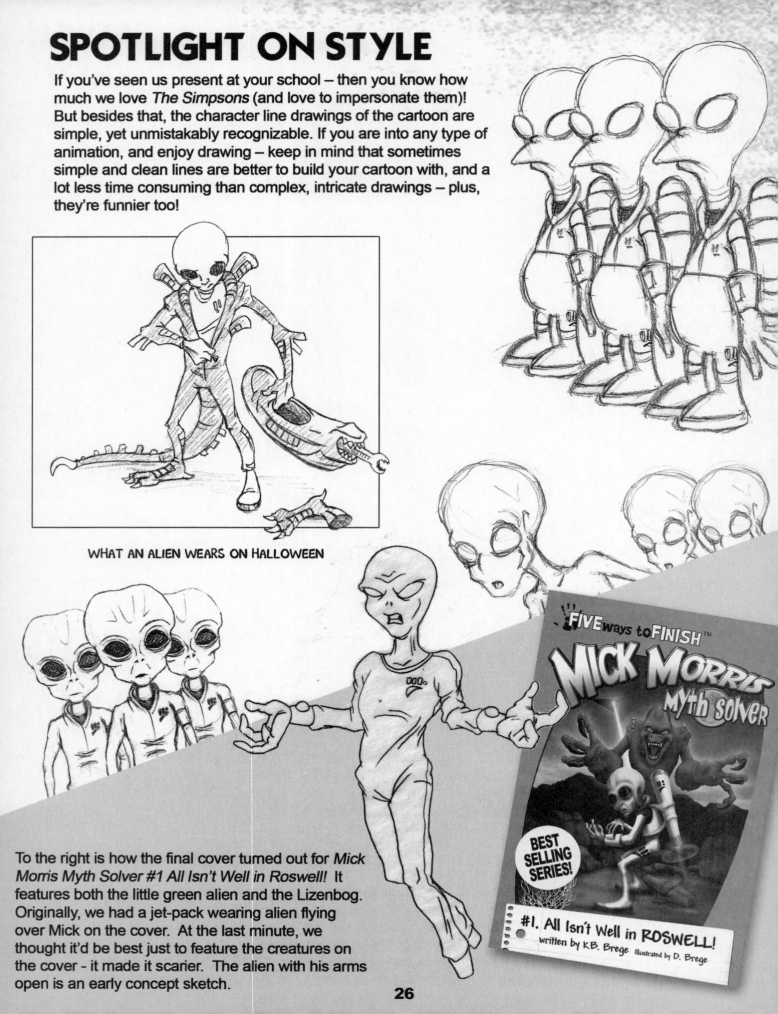

WHAT AN ALIEN WEARS ON HALLOWEEN

To the right is how the final cover turned out for *Mick Morris Myth Solver #1 All Isn't Well in Roswell!* It features both the little green alien and the Lizenbog. Originally, we had a jet-pack wearing alien flying over Mick on the cover. At the last minute, we thought it'd be best just to feature the creatures on the cover - it made it scarier. The alien with his arms open is an early concept sketch.

FIVE ways to FINISH™

Mick Morris Myth Solver

BEST SELLING SERIES!

#1. All Isn't Well in ROSWELL!
written by K.B. Brege Illustrated by D. Brege

26

LOVELAND FROG

Frogs can be cute...as long as they're not the size of a human being! Because if that were the case, their tongues could probably reach you from across a room and then slimily wrap tightly around you, sucking you into their gigantic frog mouth – YUK!!! The Loveland Frog, which was first spotted in Loveland, Ohio in 1955, was said to be a combination of a frog and a human. It was described as having a human body with hairless reptilian-leathery skin, webbed hands and feet, a huge frog-like head and enormous lips. For twenty years it went unseen until a Police Officer supposedly spotted it on his evening beat. He said that the creature was approximately 4 feet tall and a frightening half-human, half-frog creature, that walked like a human on its back legs. The Officer began to chase the creature, but when he went after it, it jumped into a nearby river – never to be seen again...that we know of. But if you ever run across a massive frog, just hope that it doesn't stick its tongue out at you!

LOVELAND, OHIO

STICK
FIGURE

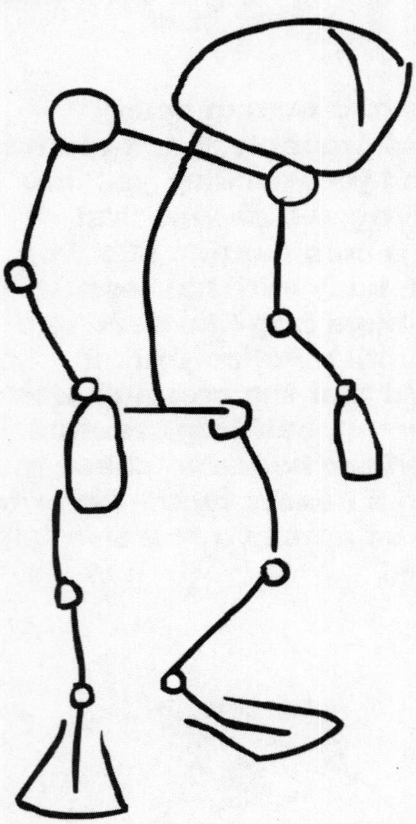

SHAPES

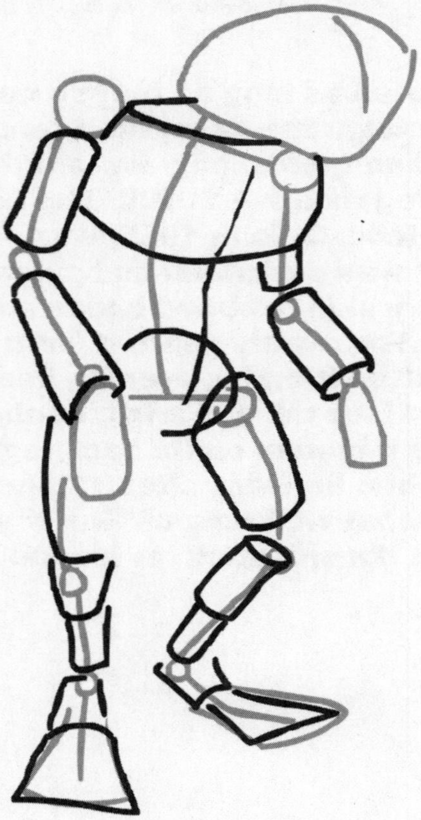

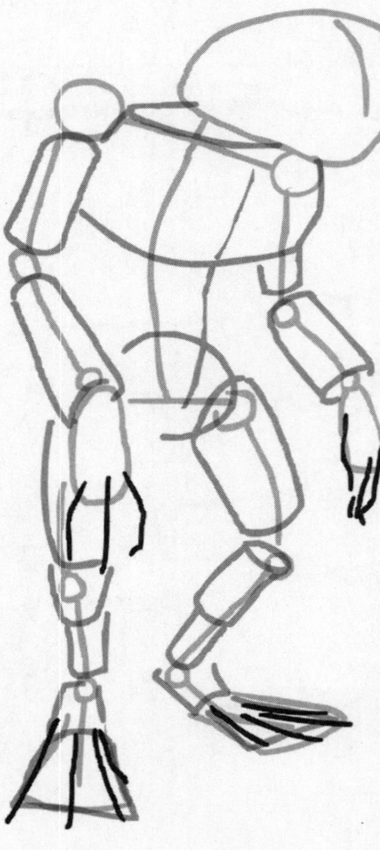

FACE BASICS
STICK FINGERS

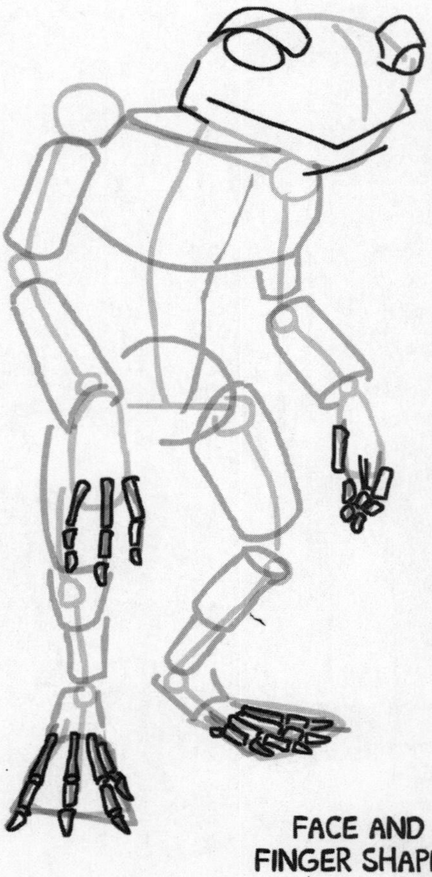

FACE AND
FINGER SHAPES

28

OUTLINE TOP
AND BOTTOM

LOVELAND FROG

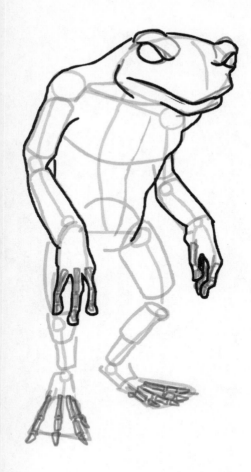

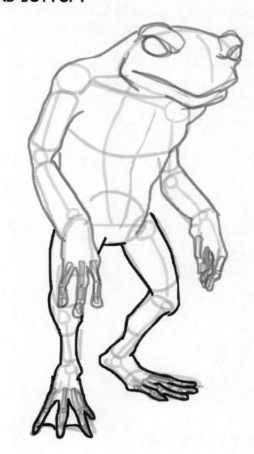

ERASE INSIDE
GUIDE LINES

EXCEPT FOR THOSE YOU'LL
NEED FOR DETAILS

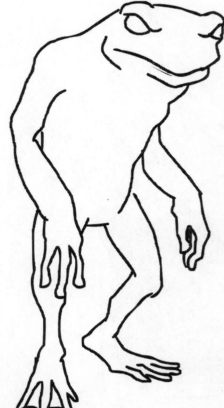

DETAIL

SPOTLIGHT ON STYLE

Pokémon, Digimon, and anime are very popular in the schools we visit. So, we decided to feature that style here… behold, the anime style Loveland Frog!

THESE TWO ARE DRIFTING OFF TO LOVELAND…

Frog legs…mmmm…I think I'll stick to chicken.

30

THUNDERBIRD

The first sighting of this enormous pre-historic looking bird was in Texas in 1890, when two cowboys shot one out of the sky, and dragged the carcass back to town. There is also a well known account in Illinois in the 1970's. Three boys were outside playing when they were suddenly chased by two gigantic birds. Two of the boys got away, but the third boy was caught when the bird clamped its massive talons into his shoulders. The boy fought and managed to get away. Another sighting was in 2002 in Alaska. These birds have been reported to be seen through history – and were a big part of Native American culture. Thunderbirds have been known to be able to create thunder and wicked storms as they fly. The scariest part of these giant birds is not just that they are known to shoot lightening out of their eyes – but that they can shapeshift into human beings! They are said to have some reptile-like features with smooth skin, wide bat-like wings and a face that resembles an alligator. They have been compared to the prehistoric Pterodactyl, as well as a Teratorn. Some argue that such large birds exist in North America...but sightings have been documented. It kinds of adds a whole new meaning to bird watching, doesn't it?

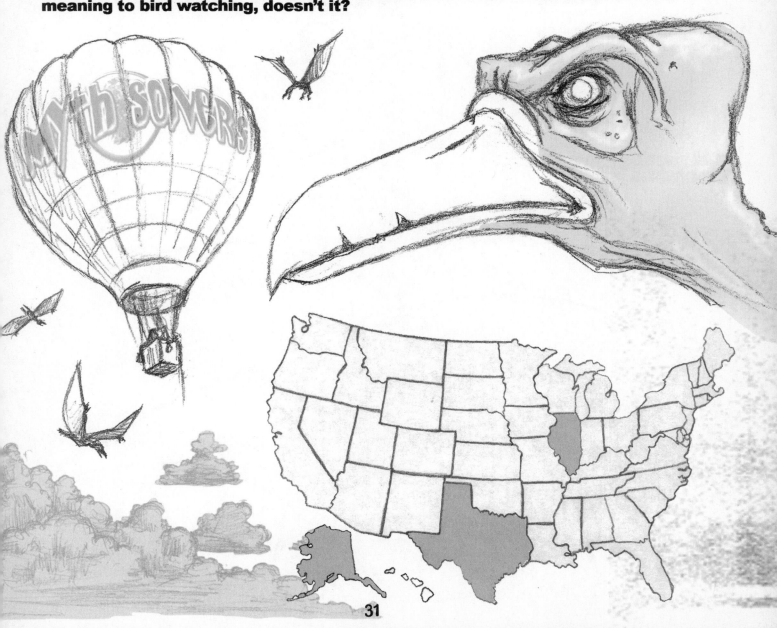

31

STICK
FIGURE

SHAPES

STICK FINGERS...
AND WINGS

FACE, WING AND
FINGER SHAPES

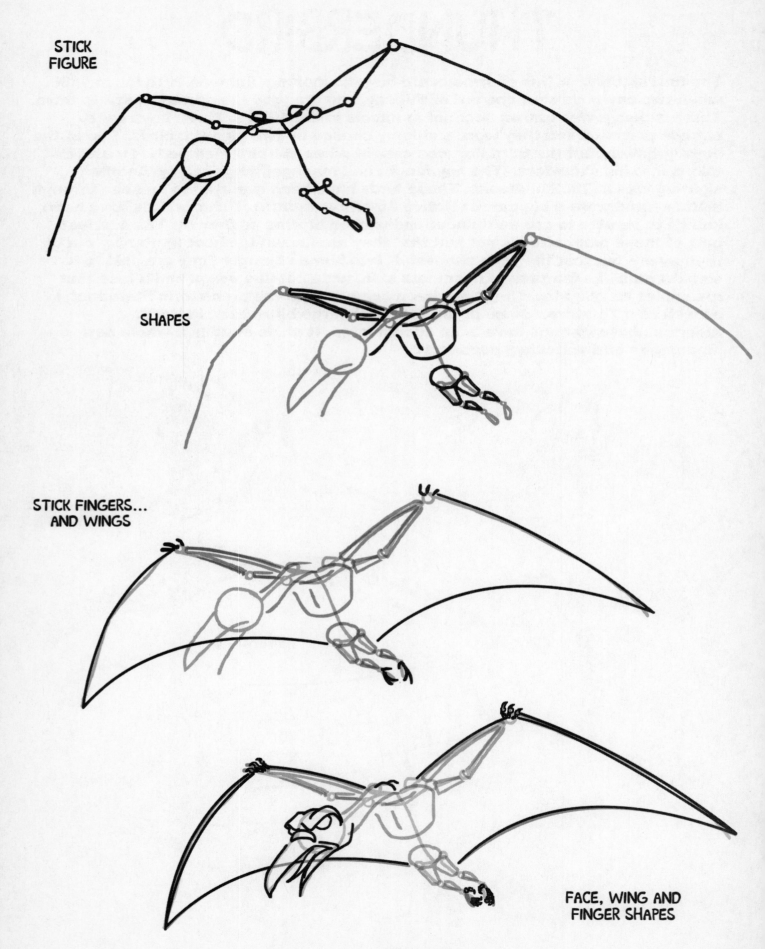

THUNDERBIRD

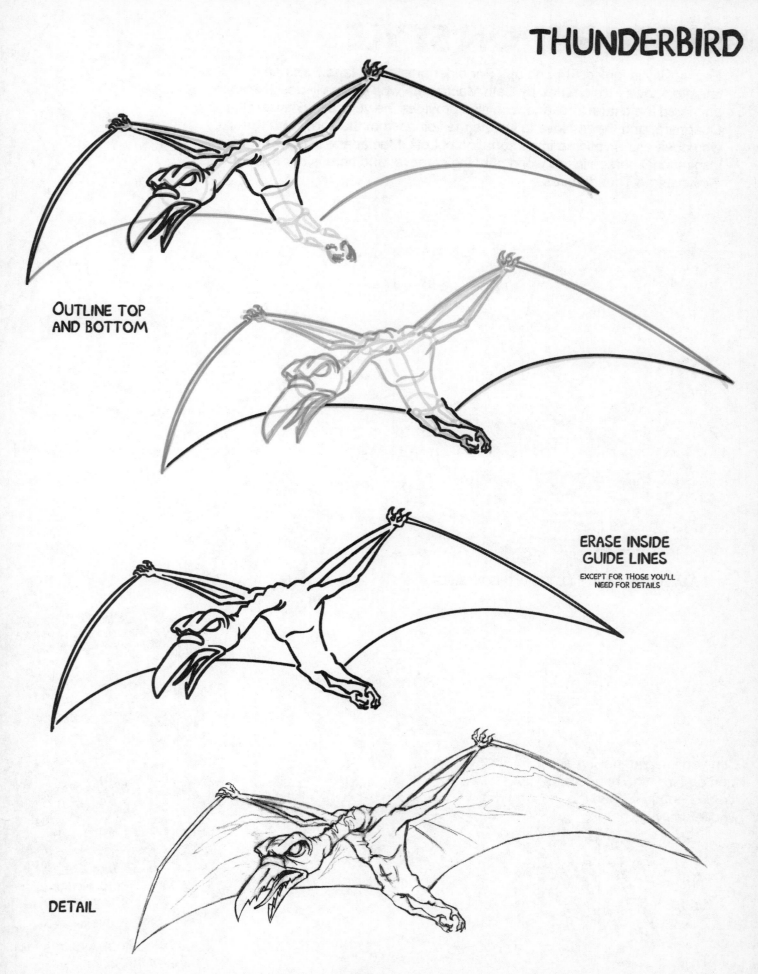

OUTLINE TOP
AND BOTTOM

ERASE INSIDE
GUIDE LINES
EXCEPT FOR THOSE YOU'LL
NEED FOR DETAILS

DETAIL

SPOTLIGHT ON STYLE

Family Guy is for kids 14 and up. For older artists and fans…it's one of my favorite shows. It's created by Seth Macfarlane who originally designed and animated the characters, and who also provides the voices of Stewie, Brian, Quagmire, and Peter. I love to imitate the voices from the show with Karen, who does and awesome impersonation of Lois. Macfarlane is truly an inspirational person in the world of being creative, and here is our *Family Guy* inspired Thunderbirds.

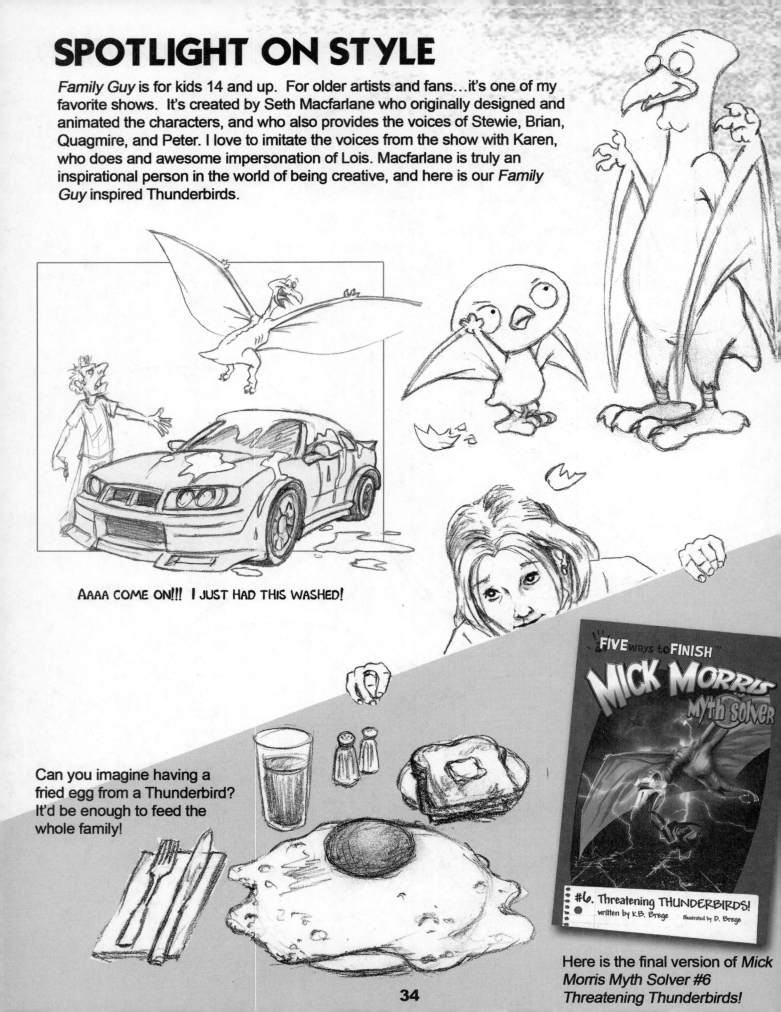

AAAA COME ON!!! I JUST HAD THIS WASHED!

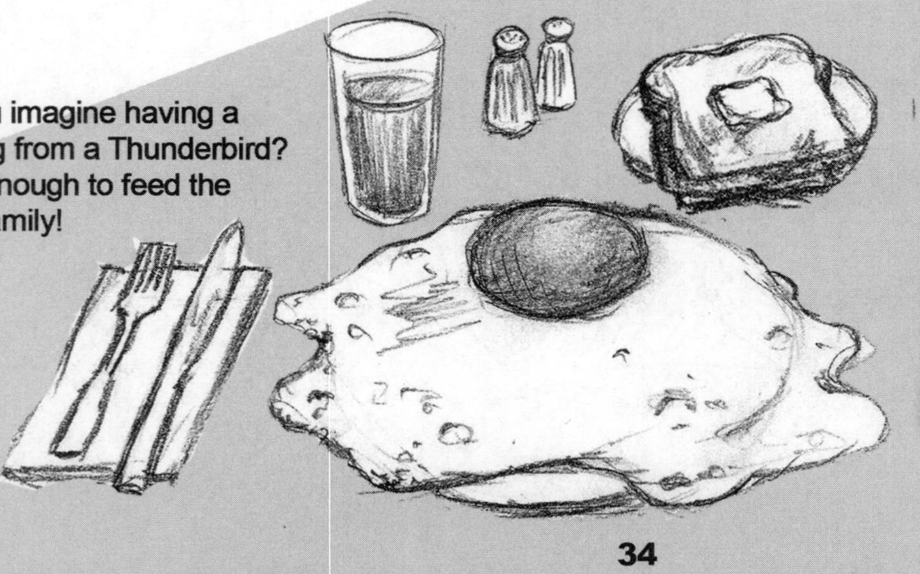

Can you imagine having a fried egg from a Thunderbird? It'd be enough to feed the whole family!

FIVE ways to FINISH™
MICK MORRIS
Myth Solver
#6. Threatening THUNDERBIRDS!
written by K.B. Brege
illustrated by D. Brege

Here is the final version of *Mick Morris Myth Solver #6 Threatening Thunderbirds!*

CRAWFORDSVILLE ATMOSPHERIC MONSTER

Here's a myth that you can tell when it's headed your way...based on a sighting in Crawfordsville, Indiana, that dates back to 1891. A loud wheezing sound and feelings of dread came over two men right before they witnessed the Crawfordsville Monster. When they looked up, they saw a terrifying phantom like creature that resembled an eel coming right at them from the clouds. Described as being over 18 feet long and about 8 feet wide with flapping fins as it squirms through the air with one glowing red eye, it makes a horrifying wheezing sound. Other people haven't been sure of what they saw when they reported the atmospheric beast; a UFO, a ghost? Either way, one day in 1891 there were 100 witnesses who insist they saw it. It is always said to be circling in the air, and sometimes swooping down towards its onlookers. This horribly frightening monster will disappear into the sky and return again. What's your guess – an apparition, a UFO, is there really a beast in the clouds? Maybe that's why the clouds always take different shapes!

CRAWFORDSVILLE, INDIANA

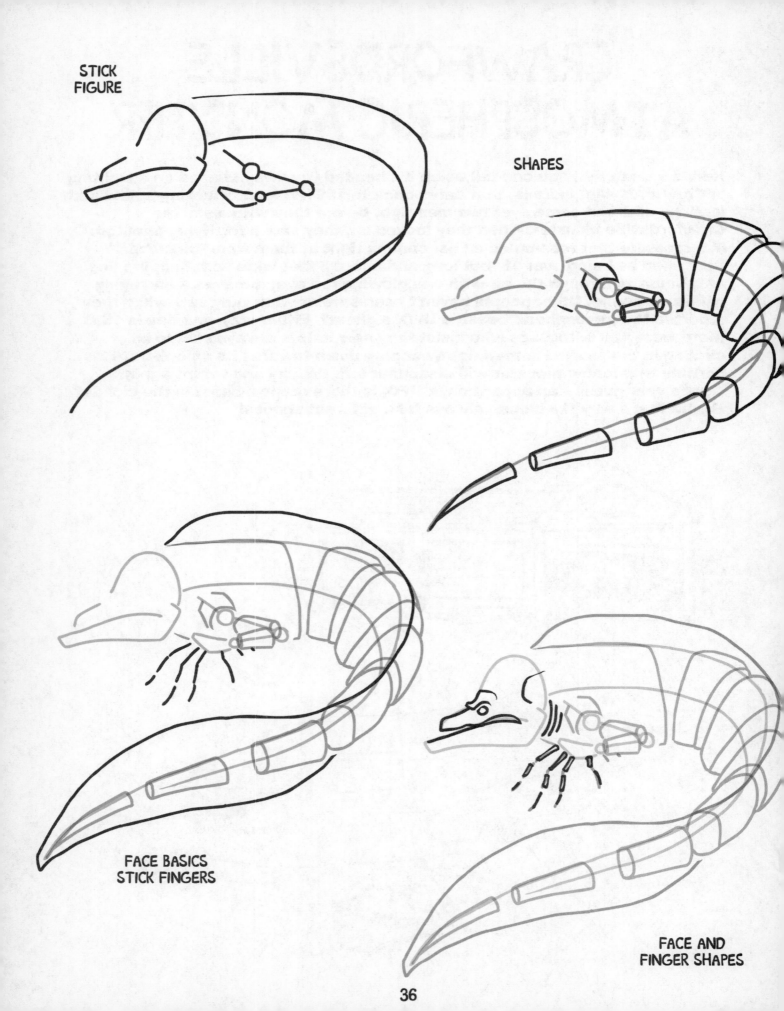

STICK
FIGURE

SHAPES

FACE BASICS
STICK FINGERS

FACE AND
FINGER SHAPES

36

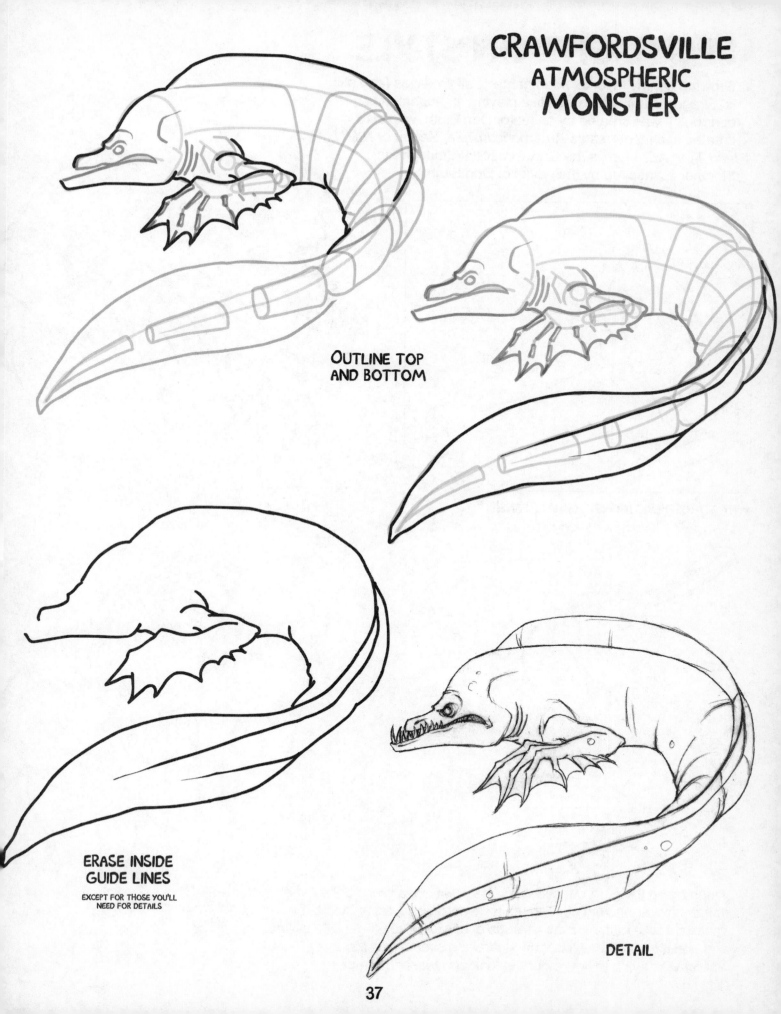

CRAWFORDSVILLE
ATMOSPHERIC
MONSTER

OUTLINE TOP
AND BOTTOM

ERASE INSIDE
GUIDE LINES

EXCEPT FOR THOSE YOU'LL
NEED FOR DETAILS

DETAIL

SPOTLIGHT ON STYLE

Growing up, my favorite video game of all time was (and still is) *Dragon's Lair*, which was like playing an animated cartoon. It was created by animator Don Bluth, who also created such features as *An American Tale, Secret of NIMH, and Titan AE*. Here is the Crawfordsville Atmospheric Monster as inspired by the works of Don Bluth.

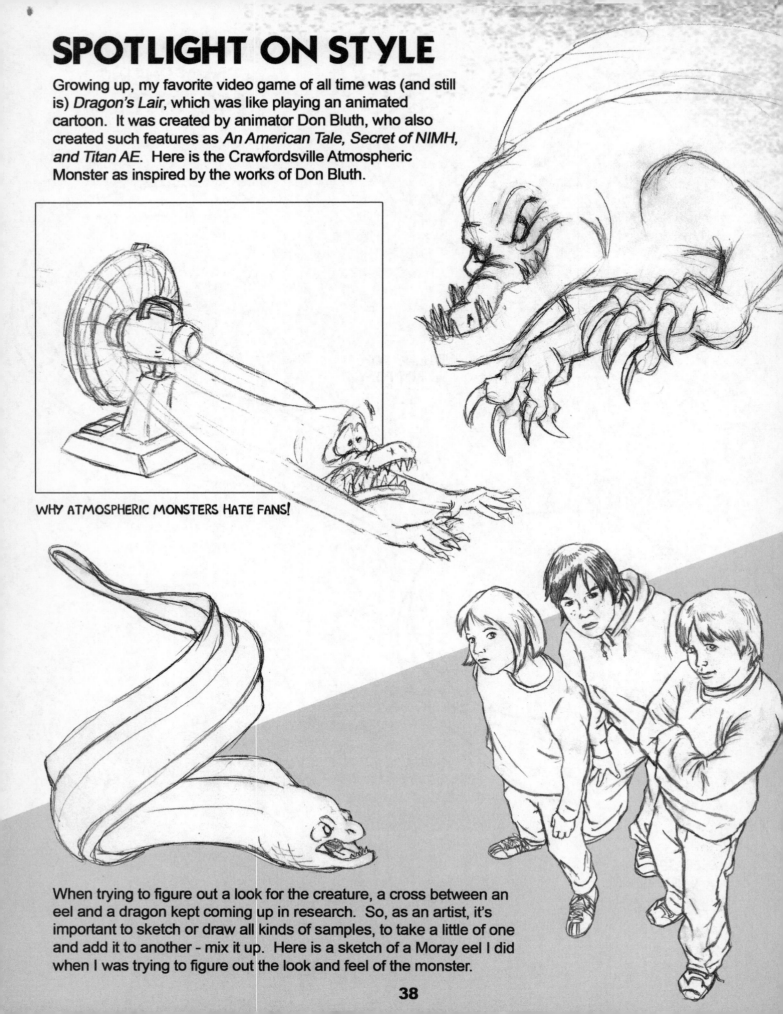

WHY ATMOSPHERIC MONSTERS HATE FANS!

When trying to figure out a look for the creature, a cross between an eel and a dragon kept coming up in research. So, as an artist, it's important to sketch or draw all kinds of samples, to take a little of one and add it to another - mix it up. Here is a sketch of a Moray eel I did when I was trying to figure out the look and feel of the monster.

38

BIGFOOT

A giant teddy bear – he's not! Bigfoot is an enormous beast who has been seen by people for hundreds of years. There is even a famous video of Bigfoot walking through the woods. In the video, as well as by those that claim they've seen him (or her) it's reported that he's a combination of human and ape; with long, thick reddish brown, or dark brown hair from head to toe, and extremely long arms with huge feet – hence the nickname "Bigfoot." He is said to be 7-10 feet tall, and weighing anywhere from 500-1000 pounds. He's supposed to be smelly, too! That's why one of his nicknames is Skunk Ape, along with some other names: Yeti, Sasquatch, Yowie and Wendigo. It's reported that this huge, ape-like creature could be a pre-historic survivor of the Gigantopithecus, which was a relation to humans over 300,000 years ago. Yikes! That's a long time to be in hiding – especially when you are so big. Lots of people say that they've discovered Bigfoot's gigantic foot prints; some have even made plaster molds of them. So, we know this beast would have a super hard time buying shoes; since the imprints that have been copied are an average of 2-3 feet in size. And, can you imagine how smelly these big feet must be? Yuck!

STICK
FIGURE

SHAPES

FACE BASICS
STICK FINGERS

FACE AND
FINGER SHAPES

BIGFOOT

OUTLINE TOP
AND BOTTOM

ERASE INSIDE
GUIDE LINES

EXCEPT FOR THOSE YOU'LL
NEED FOR DETAILS

DETAIL

SPOTLIGHT ON STYLE

Karen, Mick, and I love *The Muppets*. Jim Henson was an inspiration in so many ways. We came up with our Muppets inspired Bigfoot by adding bits and pieces from some truly memorable characters like Cookie Monster, Animal, Fozzy Bear, and a little of Sweetums. Henson's work, and his characters are timeless - he was an artistic genius.

Sketch to final art for a frame from the Comic Book ending!

FIVE ways to FINISH™
MICK MORRIS
Myth Solver

INCLUDES A COMIC BOOK ENDING

#2. BIGFOOT...BIG TROUBLE!
written by K.B. Brege Illustrated by D. Brege

Here's a sketch of Mick and Nathan as they encounter a bound and caged Bigfoot. Above is art from the comic book ending. The final cover art for *Mick Morris Myth Solver #2 Bigfoot...Big Trouble!* is on the right.

42

GREMLIN

Imagine that you are flying a plane thousands of feet up in the air when all of a sudden your instruments and devices, that help you fly, start going crazy! Immediately you are struggling to keep the plane in the air without crashing! And worst of all, there is no apparent reason why this could be happening. Countless tales, exactly like this, have been told by pilots in the military during World War II. And those pilots that made it safely back to the ground, found that their planes had been tampered with. But, when they took off their planes were in perfect working order. Thus, began the so-called myth of the Gremlins. Small furry creatures, that were extremely bad and evil, that liked to tamper with mechanical things – especially the instruments of flying planes. The word "gremlins" is described in the dictionary as, "A mischievous sprite regarded as responsible for unexplained mechanical or electrical faults." Others say that the pilots had become disoriented while flying and imagined the Gremlins, yet some pilots insisted that these furry beasts were real. Supposedly there were also good Gremlins; you could only hope that a good one was around when an evil Gremlin was playing malicious pranks on your plane – thousands of feet up in the air!

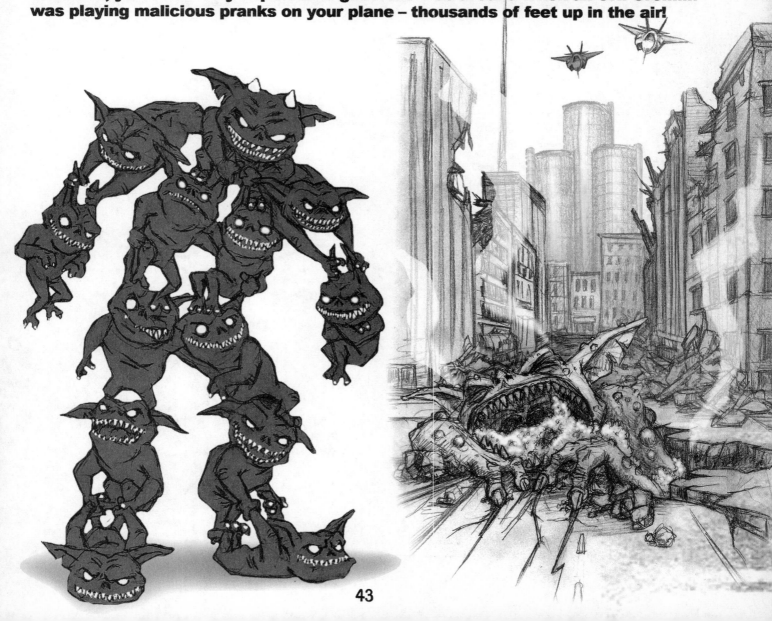

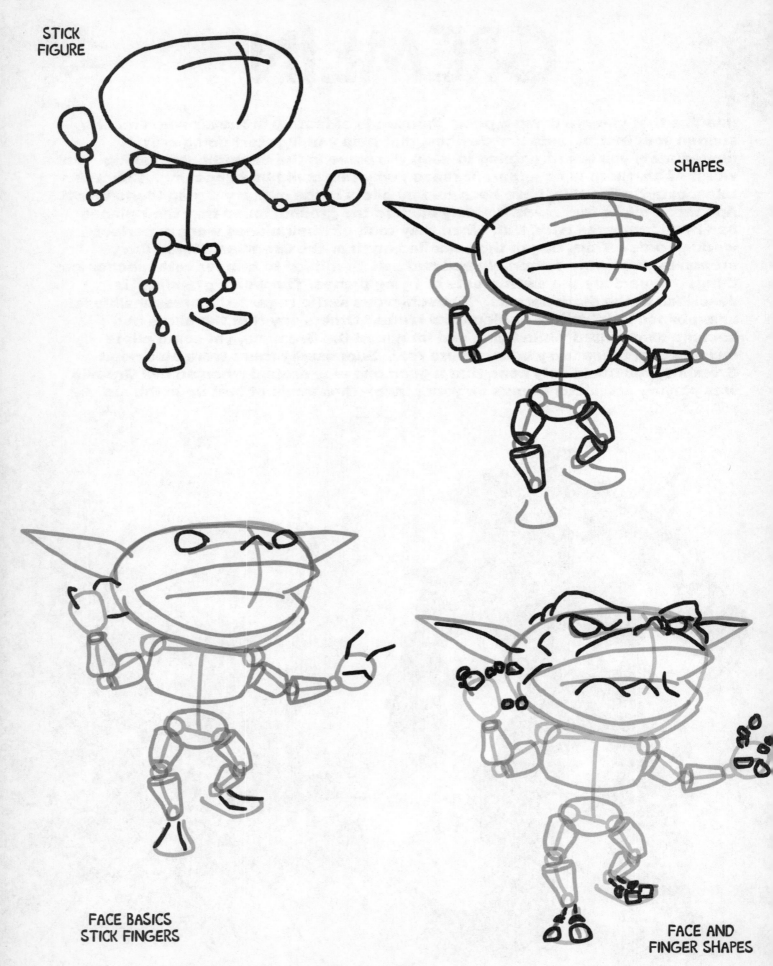

STICK
FIGURE

SHAPES

FACE BASICS
STICK FINGERS

FACE AND
FINGER SHAPES

44

GREMLIN

OUTLINE TOP
AND BOTTOM

ERASE INSIDE
GUIDE LINES

EXCEPT FOR THOSE YOU'LL
NEED FOR DETAILS

DETAIL

SPOTLIGHT ON STYLE

Charles M. Schultz was the creator of the *Peanuts* comic strip that featured Snoopy, Charlie Brown, Lucy and Linus. He later created animated television shows that still run every year: *Merry Christmas Charlie Brown*, *The Great Pumpkin Charlie Brown*. These are some of our favorites, because if they're on, we're watching. Here is our gremlin drawing inspired by a great man.

When researching *Mick Morris Myth Solver #4 Grudge of the Gremlins!*, Karen spent a lot of time at The Henry Ford museum, where this book takes place. Here you see the final cover art, as well as a sketch of one of the massive planes that's in the museum. The Henry Ford is one of our favorite museums, and if you ever get the chance - you have to visit!

FIVE ways to FINISH™

MICK MORRIS
Myth Solver

HenryFord Museu

#4. Grudge of the GREMLINS!
written by K.B. Brege Illustrated by D. Brege

46

LIZENBOG

The original myths featured in this book are easier to draw, because they have been described over and over again by countless people who claimed to have seen them. So, when we draw or write about myths, we can envision them and we have some guidelines to follow. But when it comes to having to add other creatures to our books, such as our own made up beasts, we have to be able to use our imaginations. Take for example in *Mick Morris Myth Solver #1 All Isn't Well in Roswell!*, when we needed to add evil aliens to this book we had to come up with our own version of one. We knew that it had to be different from the small aliens and it had to be very evil. We also knew we wanted a reptile type of alien - similar to those that we'd been influenced by in movies though the years. So we put our heads together and began jotting down a list of ideas. We started with a strong body with spikes on his shoulders and back, long claws, and a long tail. We decided it should have a huge head, glowing eyes and vicious teeth. We knew that we wanted it to stand on its hind legs, and we gave it thick forearms with three fingers and half a thumb – now we needed a name – the Lizenbog. Perfect! Now it's your turn, take the challenge and draw your own version of a horrifying creature – think about what would be totally scary to you, and let your imagination run wild!

STICK
FIGURE

SHAPES

FACE BASICS
STICK FINGERS

FACE AND
FINGER SHAPES

48

OUTLINE TOP
AND BOTTOM

ERASE INSIDE
GUIDE LINES
EXCEPT FOR THOSE YOU'LL
NEED FOR DETAILS

DETAIL

49

SPOTLIGHT ON STYLE

The Simpson's style returns, but this time as a Lizenbog! Both the Roswell Alien and Lizenbog are featured in our first Mick Morris book, so we thought; why not show them both in the same style? The creator of *The Simpsons* is Matt Groening, and he is someone who paved the way for prime time animation. Thank you Matt!

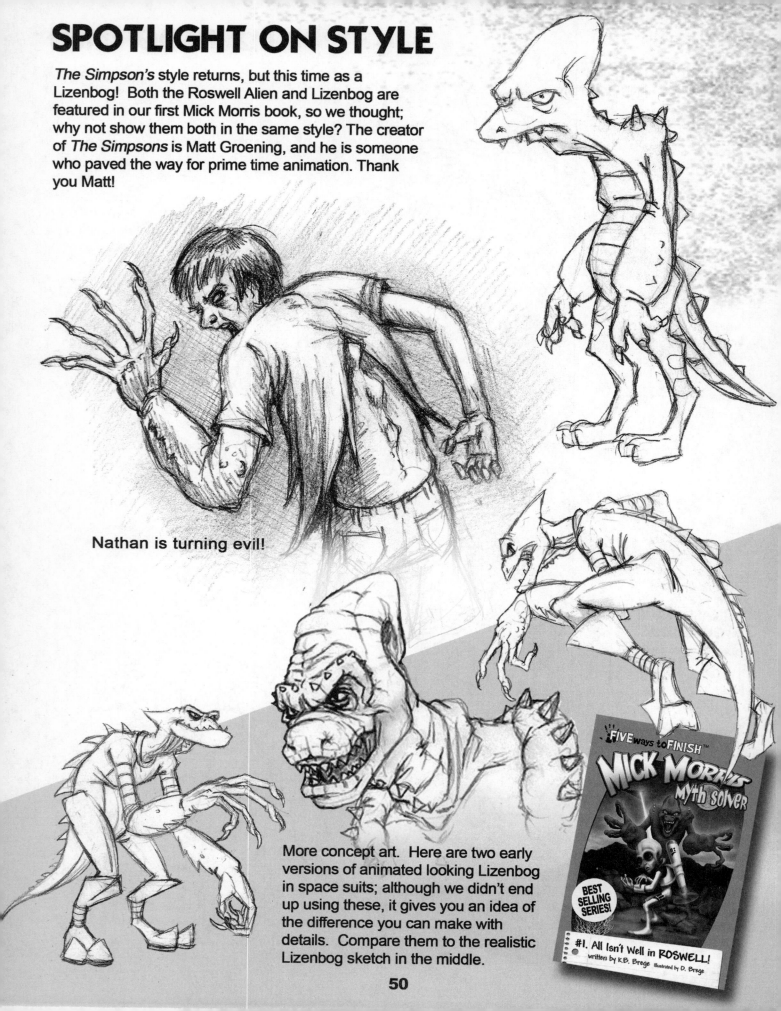

Nathan is turning evil!

More concept art. Here are two early versions of animated looking Lizenbog in space suits; although we didn't end up using these, it gives you an idea of the difference you can make with details. Compare them to the realistic Lizenbog sketch in the middle.

HODAG

This terrifying myth was first spotted in the thick woods outside of Rhinelander, Wisconsin in 1893, when it viciously lunged at a lumberjack. The lumberjack managed to save himself and blew the vicious beast up with dynamite. The second sighting of a Hodag was by a group of lumberjacks, led by the original man who saw the first Hodag. When they encountered the beast for the second time, they managed to back it into a cave and knocked it out with chloroform. When the Oneida County Fair rolled around, the live Hodag was put on display for all to see. This vicious woodland creature is supposedly a short four-legged 7-foot long beast, with a muscular body and huge dinosaur-like horns sticking out of its back, and a long spear tipped tail. It is said to have a ferocious face with a wide mouth, razor-sharp pointed teeth with enormous tusks. Even worse than it looks, it was supposed to spout flames and smoke from its nose, producing a disgusting smell. The Hodag is still a prominent symbol of Rhinelander, Wisconsin – this is one myth that will always have a place to call home.

RHINELANDER, WISCONSIN

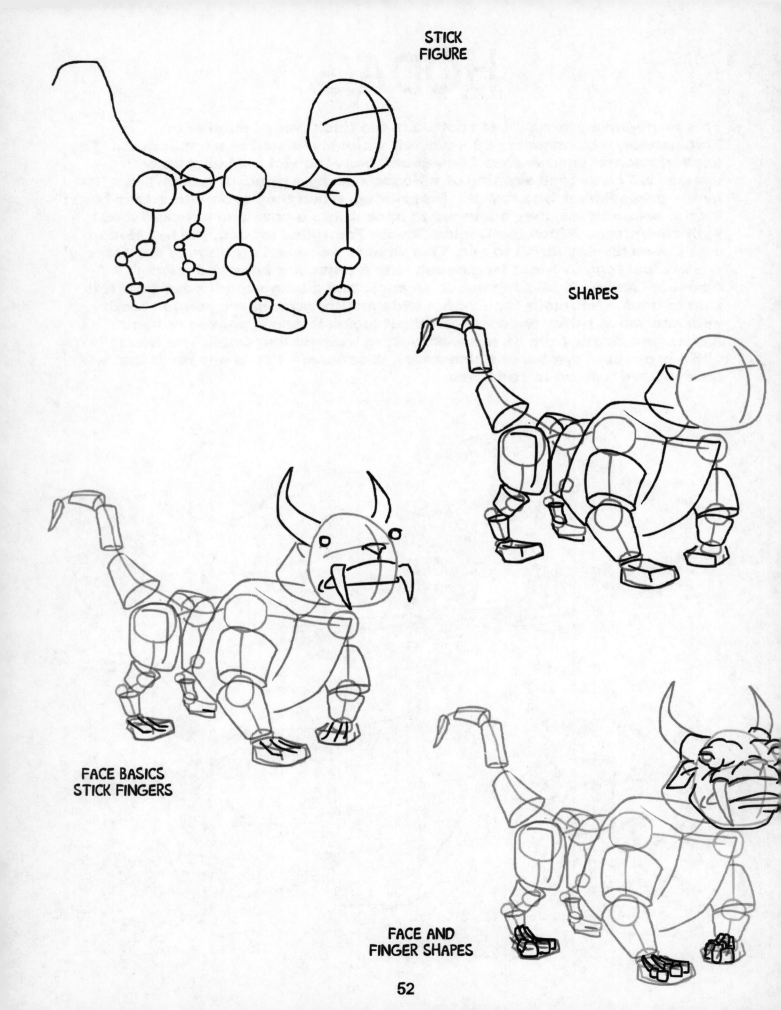

STICK
FIGURE

SHAPES

FACE BASICS
STICK FINGERS

FACE AND
FINGER SHAPES

52

HODAG

OUTLINE TOP
AND BOTTOM

ERASE INSIDE
GUIDE LINES

EXCEPT FOR THOSE YOU'LL
NEED FOR DETAILS

DETAIL

SPOTLIGHT ON STYLE

In the *South Park* cartoon, the characters are mean and mouthy; this is one cartoon that is definitely NOT for kids. But when I looked at the Hodag, something about it reminded me of angry little Eric Cartman. Here is the Hodag as if it was inspired by the works of Trey Parker and Matt Stone, the creators of the show.

HODAG HOEDOWN

This Hodag character study has a little bit of bull and walrus to it.

GOATMAN

Bahhhhh...you say to this myth, well maybe, maybe not. This cryptid is said to be 7 feet tall, half-goat and half-man with hooves and claws, is furry with goat horns sticking out of its human-like head with a goatee (apparently he doesn't shave). People claim that he is dressed in tattered clothes, and walks upright – like a human and is very wicked. Some say he has a hook for a hand. Like many of the other myths, they say he has a penchant for household pets – he eats them. Goatman was first seen in Prince Georges County, Maryland, living in an abandoned house in the back of a school yard near an old insane asylum. Many speculate on how this creature came to be. Some people say that it was from an experiment gone wrong – that a mad scientist was performing strange tests on goats...but nobody is certain. He has also been spotted in various locations in Texas and other states. Besides going after pets, Goatman is known for stalking couples. When he comes upon an innocent duo he immediately begins to harass them by throwing stones, tires or other nearby debris at them. In Maryland, there is a scary old bridge known as the "Crybaby Bridge" and it is said, that if you go there late at night you can hear the loud, shrill braying of the Goatman piercing the night air – Bahhhhh...no thanks.

MARYLAND

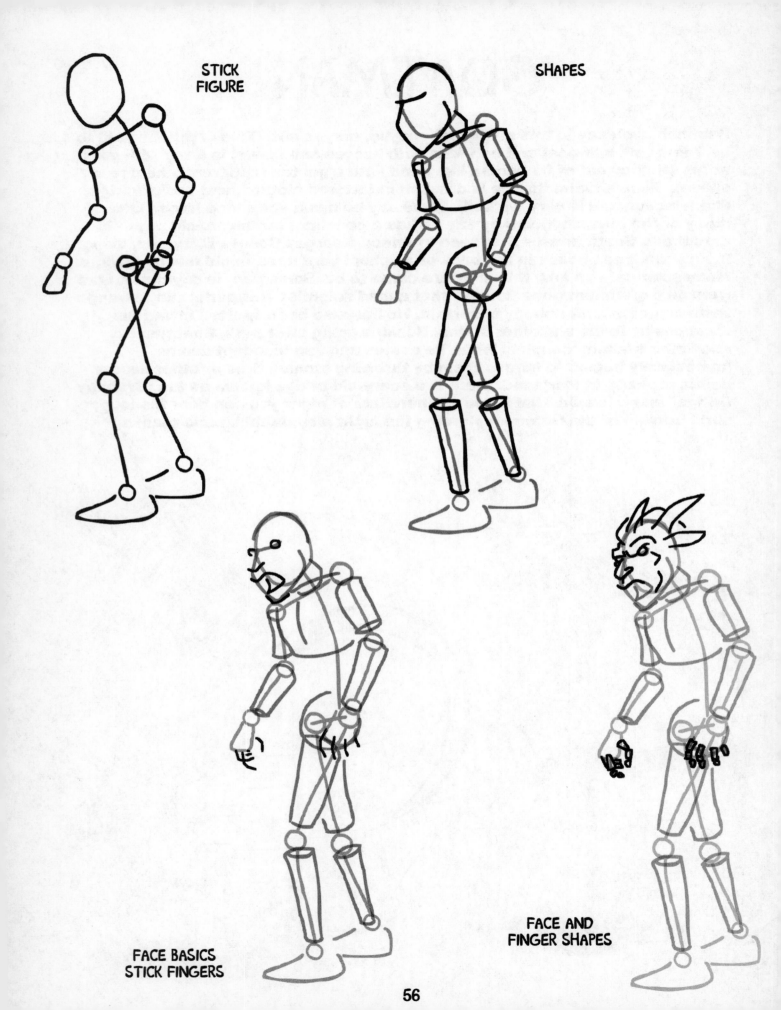

STICK
FIGURE

SHAPES

FACE BASICS
STICK FINGERS

FACE AND
FINGER SHAPES

OUTLINE TOP
AND BOTTOM

GOATMAN

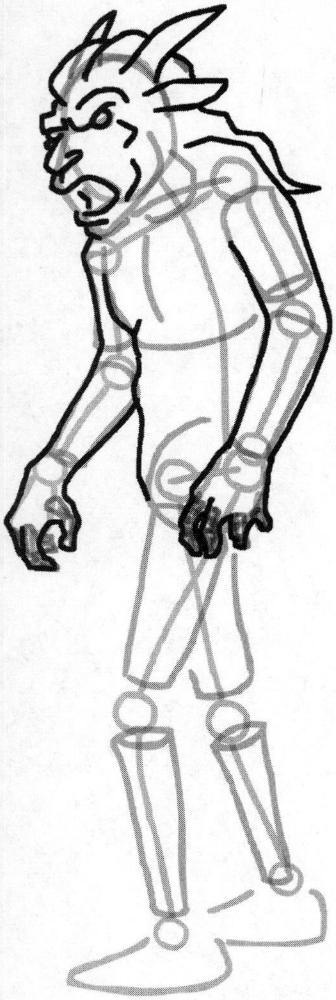

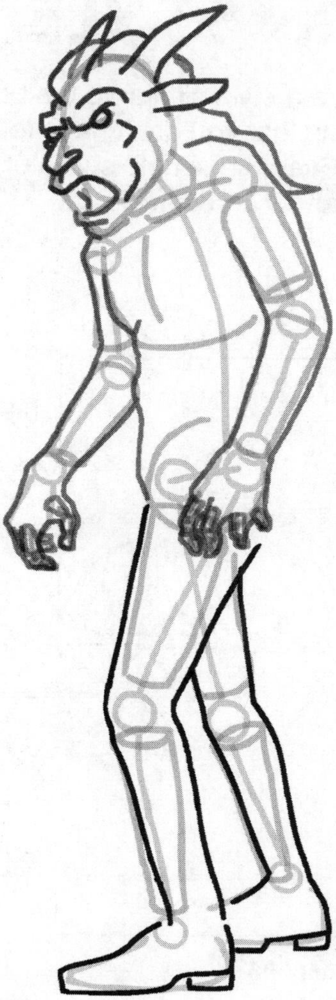

ERASE INSIDE
GUIDE LINES
EXCEPT FOR THOSE YOU'LL
NEED FOR DETAILS

DETAIL

SPOTLIGHT ON STYLE

This is where we wanted to feature a style similar to the book *Diary of a Wimpy Kid*, to show young artists that you don't have to be Leonardo da Vinci to create art. Even the simple styles of these characters are fun, effective and show emotion.

I HATE TAKING A BAAAAAAAAATH!

Early on, I wasn't sure what kind of horns to put on the Goatman. Karen and I chatted about whether they should be huge ram-type horns, or smaller, like a normal goat. So, once again, it was necessary to sketch out a ram with big horns to see how it looked. But, a ram is a sheep so it wouldn't work anyway. Ugh.

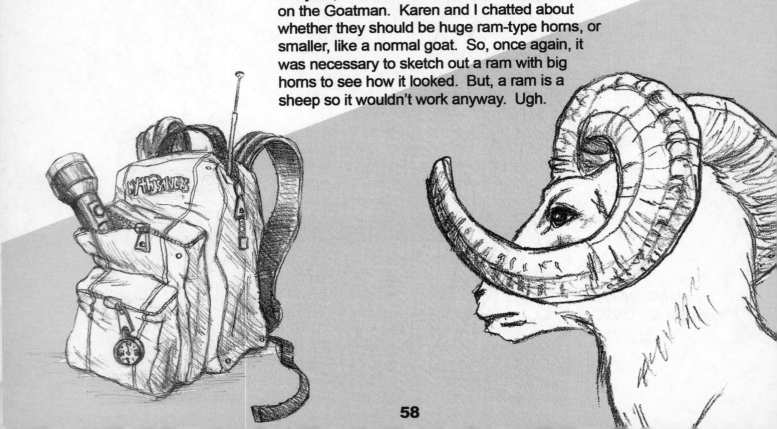

CHAMP

Samuel de Champlain, the explorer who discovered Lake Champlain in 1609, was said to be in the middle of a battle with the Native American tribe, the Iroquois. As the horrible battle took place on the shores of the lake, Champlain suddenly spotted an enormous sea serpent. I bet that would make anyone stop fighting! They never caught the giant water beast, nicknamed "Champ," as it slid back underwater. Now, hundreds of years later people are still battling over whether Champ exists or not. There have been over 240 sightings reported, and there is even a famous photograph of Champ. People describe it as an enormous type of sea serpent that resembles the Loc Ness monster. They say he is 25-30 feet in length, and has an extremely long neck. Champ has been referred to possibly being a Plesiosaurus. The funny thing about it is this lake, which runs between New York and Vermont, is very similar to the Loch Ness Lake in Scotland (you know, where the Loc Ness monster is said to exist). Both lakes are extremely long and over 300 feet deep, and both were formed in the ice age...hmmmm, kind of makes you wonder – doesn't it?

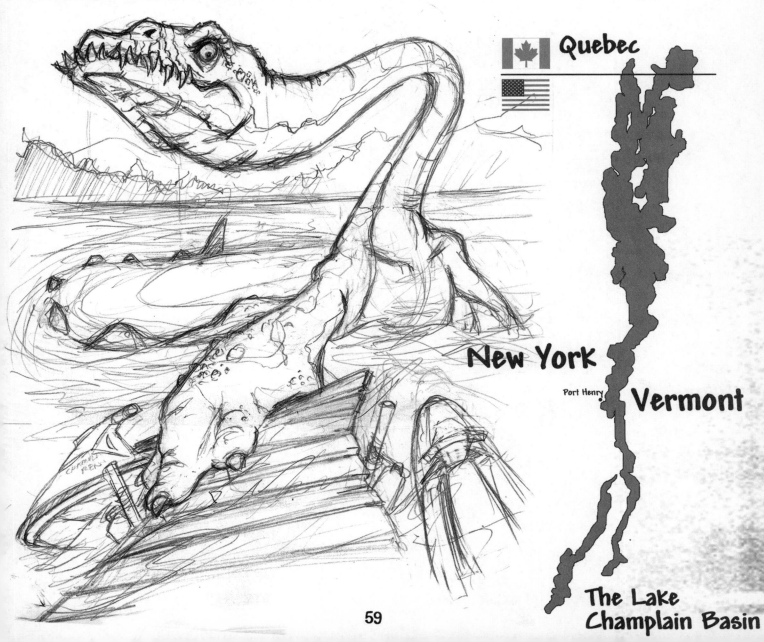

Quebec

New York

Port Henry   Vermont

The Lake
Champlain Basin

59

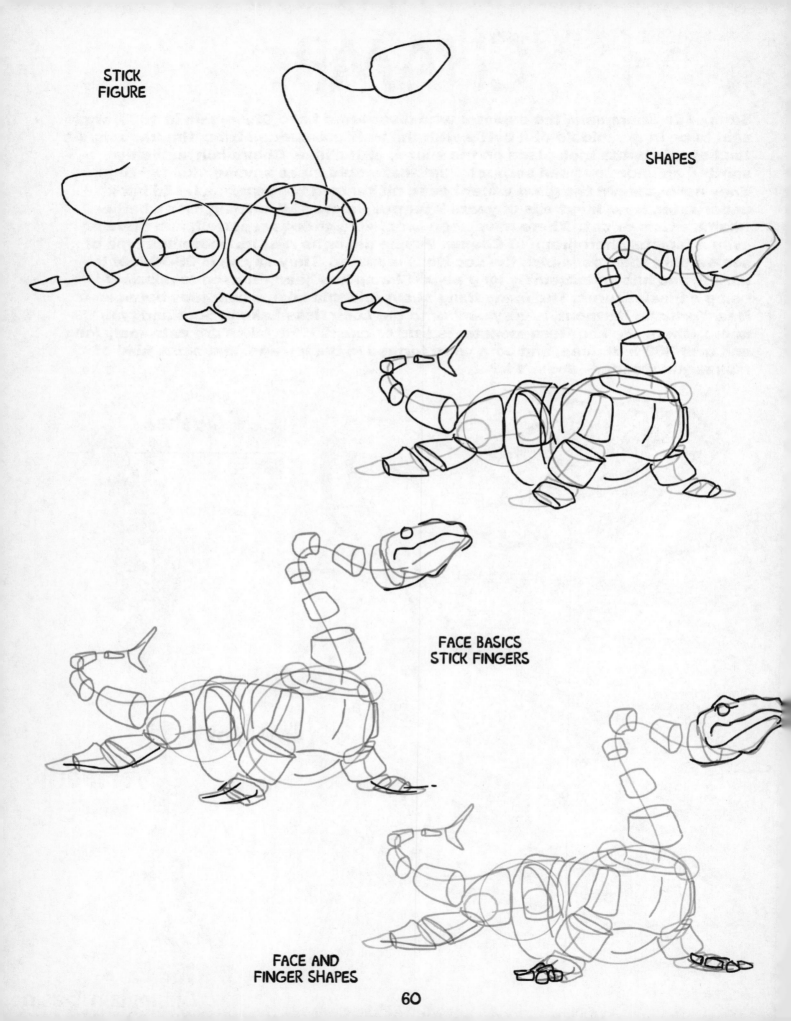

STICK
FIGURE

SHAPES

FACE BASICS
STICK FINGERS

FACE AND
FINGER SHAPES

60

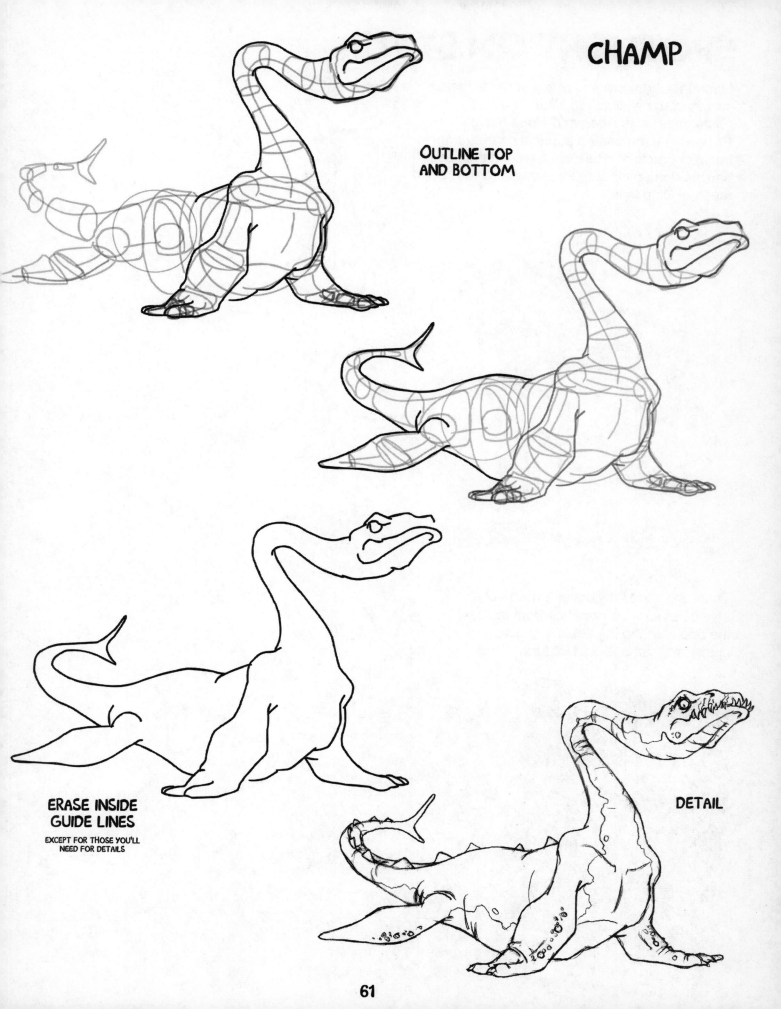

CHAMP

OUTLINE TOP
AND BOTTOM

ERASE INSIDE
GUIDE LINES

EXCEPT FOR THOSE YOU'LL
NEED FOR DETAILS

DETAIL

SPOTLIGHT ON STYLE

Hanna-Barbera created many of my favorite shows from my childhood like, *The Flintstones*, *Yogi Bear*, and *Hong Kong Phooey*. I even carried a lunchbox featuring these characters. Here we have Champ, as if he was done by them, a sea creature with a touch of Dino to it.

This is how the final cover turned out, as well as various sketches from inside the book. In the bucket is a gross chunk o' Champ. Ugh. Not tuna.

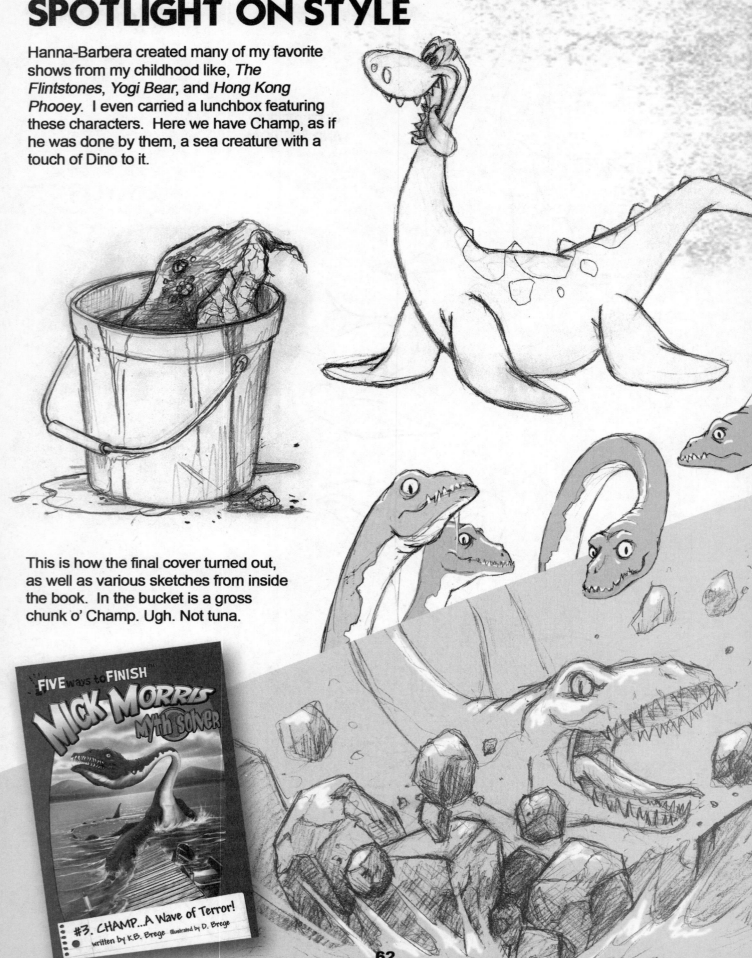

FIVE ways to FINISH

MICK MORRIS
Myth Solver

#3. CHAMP...A Wave of Terror!
written by K.B. Brege Illustrated by D. Brege

ABOMINABLE SNOWMAN

The Abominable Snowman is one of the most famous beasts in the world of cryptozoology (the study of mythical creatures). It is said that it is very similar to Bigfoot, and through the centuries has been just as elusive. Also, like Bigfoot, gigantic footprints have been found in the snow. Most of the Abominable sightings have been in the desolate regions of the Himalayas; with some sightings dating as far back as the 1800's. Many people that have scaled Mount Everest have even taken pictures of the giant footprints. This unsolvable myth was originally spotted by the people of the Himalayan region known as the Sherpas, they referred to Abominable as, "The Wild Man of the Snows." Through the years the Abominable Snowman has been classified as everything from a bear to an orangutan. Reports say that the beast weighs anywhere from 800-1000 pounds and walks upright. They say that it is covered from head-to-toe in either reddish brown or white, wiry, long hair with a huge head and enormous teeth. There have been numerous Abominable Snowman hunts, but with no luck...maybe they should consider themselves lucky.

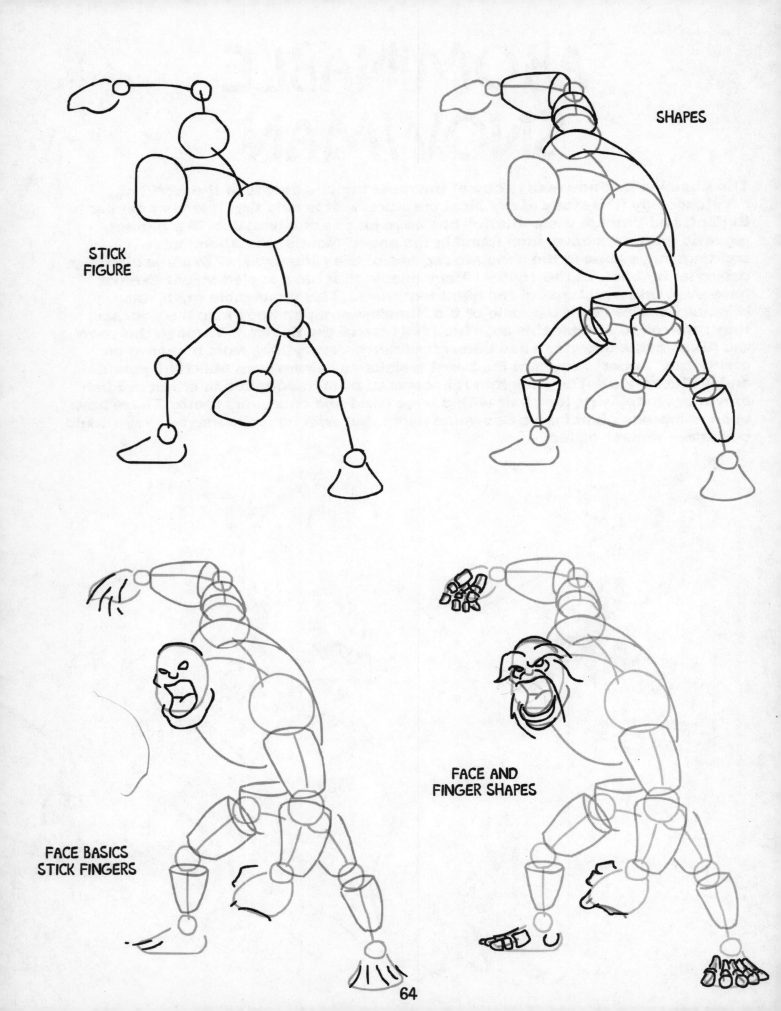

STICK
FIGURE

SHAPES

FACE BASICS
STICK FINGERS

FACE AND
FINGER SHAPES

64

OUTLINE TOP
AND BOTTOM

ERASE INSIDE
GUIDE LINES

EXCEPT FOR THOSE YOU'LL
NEED FOR DETAILS

DETAIL

SPOTLIGHT ON STYLE

What's up doc? Warner Brothers and Merrie Melodies featured some of animated cartoon's greatest characters like: Bugs Bunny, Taz, Daffy Duck, and Tweety Bird. They made me want to draw. They were very, very inspirational. As you can see here, our Abominable Snowman was inspired by the WB, with a little Taz and Gossamer (the big orange monster) in him.

SQUIRREL, CEO OF CHEESE FACTORY, GETS BONUS HE DOESN'T DESERVE!

NATIONAL
SCAR NEWS The Tabloid Ending
(Also known as newspapers that exaggerate and gossip about weird and bizarre happenings.)

STUNNING END TO THE SNOWMAN SEARCH!

$3.29 US $4.49 Canada
No charge with book purchase.

LUNCH LADY KNOCKED UNCONSCIOUS AFTER STUDENT'S GASSY ATTACK OF CAFETERIA BEANS

FIVE ways to FINISH™
MICK MORRIS Myth Solver

#5. Abominable Snowman...
A Frozen Nightmare
written by K.B. Brege   Illustrated by D. Brege

To the right is the final cover for *Mick Morris Myth Solver #5 Abominable Snowman…A Frozen Nightmare!*. Here is an unused early cover painting. As Karen said, "That one doesn't look mean enough – let's make it scarier." I couldn't agree with her more.

66

CHUPACABRA

This beast likes pets and livestock – for dinner that is! And especially goats! Hundreds of animal killings by this unknown myth have been reported across the United States from Maine to Texas since the early 1930's, and the only explanation is some kind of vicious beast named Chupacabra. The name itself translates from Spanish to "goat-sucker." It has been described as being a mix of a hairless dog with a long snout, a vicious rat-look, and a body shape similar to that of a kangaroo, with short front legs and long back legs. It is also said to have large fang-like teeth and vampire tendencies – a.k.a. bloodsucker! That's right they say it drains the blood out of its victims. People, that insist they've found a corpse of a Chupacabra, say it's more like a reptile with grayish-green scales and sharp, long, pointy spines running down its back. It's said to stand on its hind legs, and is 3-4 feet tall with enormous eye sockets, fangs and claws. The varieties of descriptions are endless, but it is always described as dog-like. Many people think it's an alien, while others say that it's just a vicious, wild dog. Either way, watch your goats and keep your pets in for dinner!

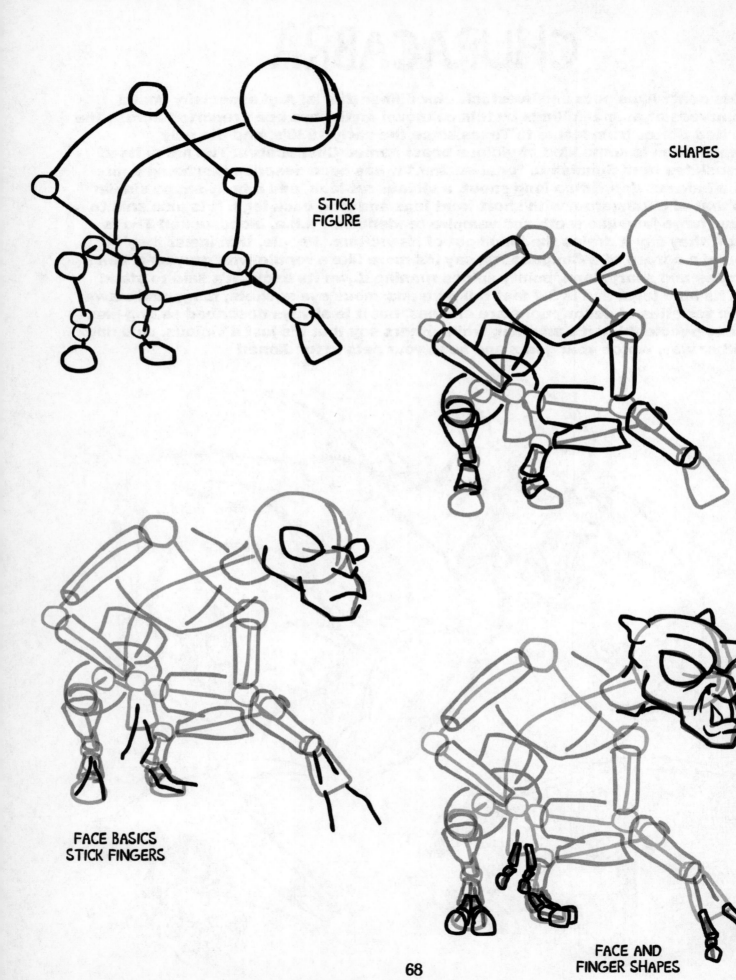

STICK FIGURE

SHAPES

FACE BASICS
STICK FINGERS

FACE AND
FINGER SHAPES

68

CHUPACABRA

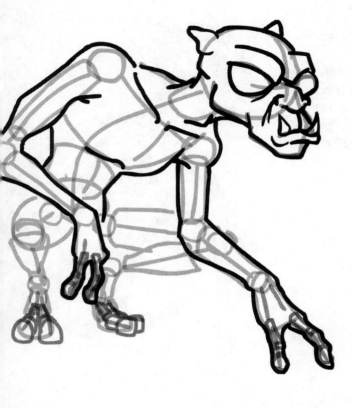

OUTLINE TOP
AND BOTTOM

ERASE INSIDE
GUIDE LINES

EXCEPT FOR THOSE YOU'LL
NEED FOR DETAILS

DETAIL

SPOTLIGHT ON STYLE

Walt Disney started way back in 1928 with Mickey Mouse as Steamboat Willy, and an empire was born by an entertainment genius and visionary. Here is our Chupacabara as if it could've appeared in a classic animated Disney Cartoon. I can't even imagine our world without what Disney created. And his legacy lives on, continuing to entertain and make us smile. If you ever feel like you can't do something…just remember this famous quote from Walt Disney, "It's kind of fun to do the impossible."

CHALUPACABRA
DON'T FORGET THE SALSA!

What is Chupacabra's favorite food? Goats! And we aren't talking feta cheese here – gross! Here is a concept sketch of one ready to dine.

JERSEY DEVIL

The New Jersey Devil (also called the Leeds Devil) is a frightening myth that has been around since the1700's, with many, many stories from people who have actually encountered it. They say that it has haunted the New Jersey Pine Barrens for over 260 years – terrorizing anyone who enters the dark, swampy forest. Although, there are several accounts of it being killed – it always returns, which would mean it's immortal. Nobody knows for sure how the Jersey Devil came to be. Although, there are numerous stories, the one that seems to stand out the most is that a devil was born into the Leeds or Shroud family in Leeds Point, New Jersey. This scary creature is said to have a serpentine body with hair and feathers all over it, enormous bat wings, and a gnarled face on a horse's head. Its eyes are supposedly glowing red, and it has deer-like antlers, hoofed feet, talon-like claws, and a long forked tail. It is known to make horrible high-pitched screaming or hissing sounds when it is seen looming over various parts of New Jersey. This beast has been said to terrorize and devour livestock and track humans. There have also been accounts of strange hoof shaped tracks that have been found...but the weirdest thing about these devilish prints is that they can go up buildings and trees and then suddenly disappear. Which would explain that this beast really is able to fly. But, if the New Jersey Devil does exist, it likes its home in the Pine Barrens, and I would suggest you let it be.

NEW JERSEY

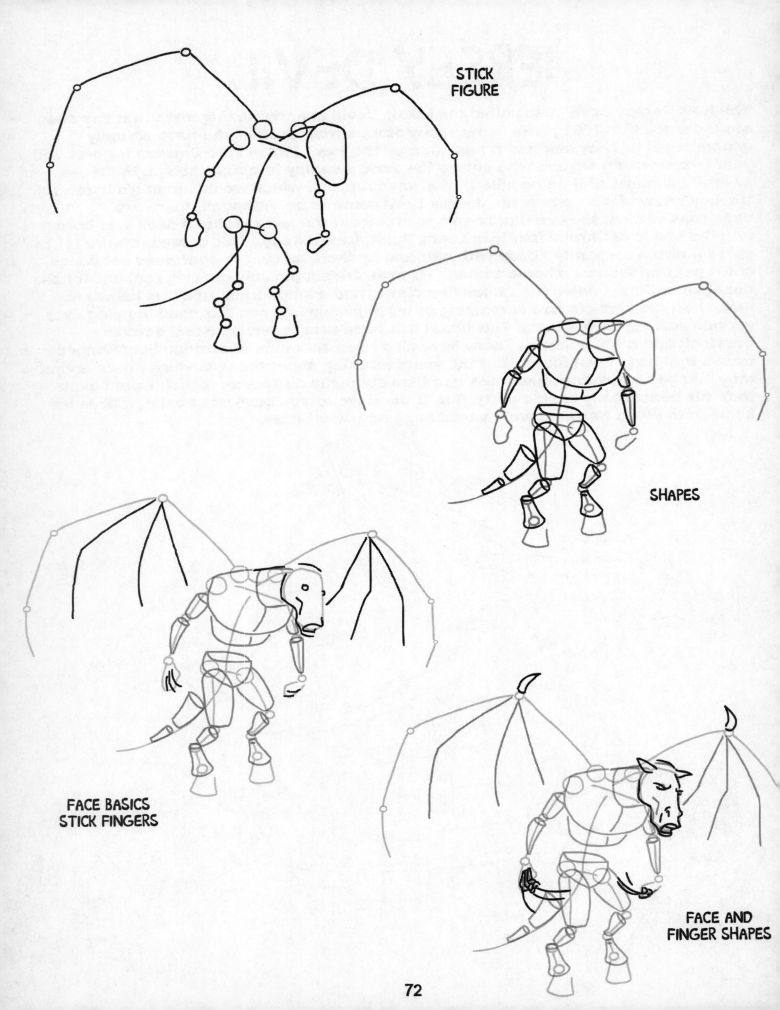

STICK
FIGURE

SHAPES

FACE BASICS
STICK FINGERS

FACE AND
FINGER SHAPES

72

JERSEY DEVL

OUTLINE TOP
AND BOTTOM

ERASE INSIDE
GUIDE LINES

EXCEPT FOR THOSE YOU'LL
NEED FOR DETAILS

DETAIL

SPOTLIGHT ON STYLE

Universal Studios put out some classic cartoons starring fantastic characters like Bullwinkle and Rocky, and Boris and Natasha. They are some of our favorites. Interesting Fact: Karen and I had the opportunity to provide voice imitations for animated *Bullwinkle* and *Fractured Fairy Tales* storybooks. Here is the Jersey Devil inspired by the style of those classics.

DJ JERSEY D

As you know by now, we like to make things scary, so we had come up with the idea of putting a skull head on the Jersey Devil. Oh yeah, read about this guy and get ready to pull the covers over your head at night.

GREAT JOB! FOR ALL OF YOUR WONDERFUL LEARNING AND DRAWING - HERE'S YOUR BONUS: A VAMPIRE CAT!

That's right, we're they type of people who like to give presents! So for being such an artistic person, we want you to have this ferocious feline. You get your very own four page breakdown on how to draw this ancient Japanese legend. All you have to do is email us at: **staff@teambcreative.com** and we'll send it to you (in a PDF format – be sure to add us to your contacts so that you get it). Petting this pretty kitty could be very dangerous, better to just draw, or write about it.

WORKING WITH A WRITER - HE SAID/ SHE SAID:

Darrin: When it comes to working as an artist in the world of books, you will almost always (unless it is your book-alone, and you are the sole author, and you plan on publishing it yourself) have to follow the direction of someone else, and what their vision and look of the book is.

Karen: This is true, but we find that one of the best parts of the book art is finding ourselves coming together with the same vision…sometimes it's like we read each other's minds…ouuuuu scary!

Darrin: Yeah, it freaks us out sometimes…But we have heard of cases where the artist and the author never even get to chat – usually when a major publishing house has taken over, and then it is their vision.

Karen: Oh, that would be sad…because for our books, it's always our imaginations combined, author and illustrator making up the true style and feel of the book – be it the cover or the drawings inside.

Darrin: Okay, so I guess what we are trying to tell you, is to always make sure that you have some control over your artwork, and to be able to chat with the person whose original vision it is. Work things out together and discuss it – that is very important for the sake of the book.

Karen: Yep. So important! Oh! And we should also tell them to never-ever-ever use someone else's work, without getting their permission first.

Darrin: Correct.

Karen: Anything else?

Darrin: Yeah, what do you think about the cover for the next book?

Karen: Well, what do you think of…

#1 All Isn't Well in ROSWELL!
ISBN: 978-0-9774119-0-0

#2 BIGFOOT...BIG TROUBLE!
ISBN: 978-0-9774119-1-7

#3 CHAMP...A Wave of Terror!
ISBN: 978-0-9774119-2-4

#4 Grudge of the GREMLINS!
ISBN: 978-0-9774119-3-1

#5 Abominable Snowman...
A Frozen Nightmare!
ISBN: 978-0-9774119-4-8

#6 Threatening THUNDERBIRDS!
ISBN: 978-0-9774119-8-6

THIS IS A VERY IMPORTANT MESSAGE...IT IS NOT A TEST... I REPEAT, IT IS NOT A TEST...SO PLEASE DON'T TOUCH THAT DIAL

You know we think that it's totally cool that you are into drawing and art, but (and that's a big but) we really want to make sure that you know the importance of reading, too. Because no matter what your interests are, whether you are into art, sports, or cooking (we love food) we know that in order to be successful YOU HAVE TO BE A GOOD READER!!! And although we like to joke around, the two of us would never have the awesome careers that we do – if we weren't good readers. Because no matter what you do in life – you have to be able to read! Do you get that? So, follow your heart and your dreams...but along the way make sure that you find books or magazines that interest you and read. It will make a GI-NOURMOUS difference in your life! We promise – READ ON!!!

There ARE Monsters in America...

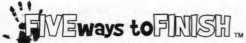

Interactive reading is back! Each Mick Morris Myth Solver book features Five Ways to Finish™ or five different endings. There are always a normal and scary ending, but the other endings will change. You'll find everything from a sci-fi ending, to comic book, western, talk show & more!

Get your Mick Morris Myth Solver books at your local bookstore, or for an autographed copy order at www.mickmorris.com.

Two for One, Author & Illustrator

The Breges have an outstanding high-energy, fun, edu-tainment presentation for schools, libraries, organizations and associations. If you would like more information email: karen@teambcreative.com.

Your interactive presentation was just as amazing as your interactive books-that I cannot keep on my shelves!
Denise Brandt, Elementary School Media Specialist, Bloomfield, MI.

It was obvious that their act was a smash by the line of smiling faces waiting for an autograph, picture or book purchase at the end. When looking for an act that will inspire, empower and entertain children, you can't go wrong with the Breges.

Pat Slater, Head Librarian Children's Services Redford, MI.

It was a happy day for us, made happier with your charm, talent, and great humor. Your creative team, Darrin, Karen and Mick won our hearts. We had lots of fun, and we learned so much about the craft. Delightful.
Beatrice Catherino, Distinquished Emeritus, Department of English, Oakland Community College.

Our students are still asking for your books in the library. I can't keep them on the shelves at all. You two were fabulous, engaging, exciting and fun. I will be sure to recommend you to every school I can think of.
Shari Andrus, Media Specialist, Cedar View Elementary.

We saw you at the Clinton-Macomb Library and became instant fans. Your message about reading and working hard and practicing is just what kids need! Your entusiasm is infectious! You guys are great!
A Mom, Macomb Township, MI

I hope you make some more new books. They were great! I would like to know you better!
Elementary Student, Toledo, OH.

We felt that this program was well worth hosting at our library. It was age appropriate for the children, while still being entertaining for the adults. It was fast-paced and sustained the audiences attention. Patrons complimented us on the Breges' appearance and we plan to have them back again.

Margi Karp-Opperer, Department Head

Your presentation had something for all ages, What a great opportunity for them to see real life authors and artists, interact with them, and hear for themselves how they could be writers and artists too!
Tom Priest, Principal, St. John Vianney Schoo

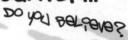

79

THANK YOU FELLOW ARTISTS!
KEEP UP THE GOOD WORK!